THE FORGIVING COMMUNITY

The FORGIVING COMMUNITY

by
William Klassen

THE WESTMINSTER PRESS
Philadelphia

LIBRARY OF CONGRESS CATALOG CARD No. 66–10141

Published by The Westminster Press ⊕
Philadelphia, Pennsylvania

PRINTED IN THE UNITED STATES OF AMERICA

Preface

The subject of forgiveness frequently comes to the surface as one works with people in the church. It has been my good fortune to teach the New Testament to seminary students, to be permitted to listen to the concerns of some troubled people, and to spend a year at the Menninger Foundation in Topeka, Kansas, as a theological fellow. In Topeka, with its unlimited opportunity for clinical observation and involvement, the various dimensions of the subject of forgiveness were first opened up to me.

It would be unkind indeed not to make my debt to the various men there a matter of public record. Thomas Klink, chaplain and coordinator of the program in religion and psychiatry, patiently introduced me to the intricacies of the clinical programs at Topeka and also did everything within his power to make the stay of the theological fellows a pleasant and profitable one. Paul Pruyser, Ph.D., director of education at the Menninger Foundation, a distinguished lecturer in the field of psychology of religion, a brilliant clinical psychologist, and, above all, a sympathetic listener to all the concerns of the theologians added an indispensable dimension to our program. As an active member of the church and a fervent wrestler with the issues in religion and psychiatry, his integrity gave me courage to believe that syncretism is not necessary to gain some degree of resolution of the issues. Seward Hiltner's monthly visits from the ivied towers of Princeton were also of great value.

On the clinical side, my greatest debt is to Mitchell Jones, M.D., the medical director of Prairie View Hospital, Newton, Kansas. The administrator, Elmer Ediger, and other members of the staff made my monthly visits there a rich learning experience. Another medical director, Otto Klassen, M.D., of the Oaklawn Psychiatric Center, Elkhart, Indiana, has given unsparingly of his time to discuss some of the issues raised herein and become thereby a "friend closer than a brother."

Stimulation and support for the writing have also come from the seminaries where I have taught. To President Erland Waltner, of Mennonite Biblical Seminary, Elkhart, Indiana, who graciously provided a leave for me during the year, 1961–1962, and to the dean of New York Biblical Seminary, Norman Baxter, whose sensitivity to reasonable teaching loads provided me with the time to complete this volume, I express my thanks. Without the courteous assistance of the staff at Robert E. Speer Library, Princeton Theological Seminary, my work would have been impossible, or at least much more difficult. Millard Lind, Goshen Seminary, read proofs and gave many helpful suggestions.

Finally, to my wife, Marilyn, who has patiently typed the manuscript a number of times and who has so graciously demonstrated the truth of the words of H. R. Macintosh that "it is in the home that the profound and beautiful and creative meaning of 'forgiveness' is first learnt," I dedicate these labors.   W. K.

Contents

Contents

Abbreviations

CD	Damascus Document
ET	*The Expository Times*
HTR	*Harvard Theological Review*
IDB	*The Interpreter's Dictionary of the Bible*
JBL	*Journal of Biblical Literature*
NEB	*The New English Bible*
NTD	*Das Neue Testament Deutsch*
NTS	*New Testament Studies*
RGG	*Die Religion in Geschichte und Gegenwart* (3d edition)
1QS	Manual of Discipline
1QpHab	Habakkuk Commentary
SE	Standard Edition (Works of Sigmund Freud)
TWNT	*Theologisches Wörterbuch zum Neuen Testament*, edited by G. Friedrich
ZnW	*Zeitschrift für die neutestamentliche Wissenschaft*

Introduction

How is it possible to write a book on forgiveness? It is impossible.[1]—*Charles Williams.*

The important place of forgiveness in the life of the church is generally admitted. Whether one looks at the Old or the New Testament, it is clear that the literary material from which Christianity draws its inspiration presents forgiveness as one significant aspect in man's relationship to God. The miracle of forgiveness has also emerged repeatedly in the history of the Christian church. In a very real sense, the great victories in the history of the church have been those occasions when forgiveness was newly discovered and applied to the sense of sin that permeated either the individual or the culture in which he lived. There would have been no Reformation without Luther's experience of forgiveness before God. Wesley's great contribution to Christianity was made after he had become joyfully aware that God had forgiven him.

The theme of forgiveness has been competently dealt

with in the past; with greatest competence and distinction by H. R. Mackintosh.[2] Yet each aspect of the gospel, no matter how familiar, demands restudying in each generation. Several reasons make a study of forgiveness imperative for us today.

First, we are witnessing renewed interest in Bible study. A variety of reasons has brought this about, not the least of which is the conviction that God has a message for us in the Holy Scriptures, which we disparage to our own loss. Modern Biblical scholars have not arrived at a consensus on the extent to which, and precisely how, the Bible is the inspired Word of God, and only in a few instances have the older clichés and formulations been transcended. Nevertheless, the various theological communions are listening to the words of Holy Scripture in a more serious mood than they did fifty years ago.

This treatment of forgiveness attempts to wrestle with the Biblical understanding of forgiveness before we do anything else. The concern is not to be in step with, or attach ourselves to, the "new Biblical theology" and merely to follow the trends. Creativity and vitality in church life and elsewhere do not generally result from following trends. Rather, our study of the Scriptures is a product of the conviction that wherever God has charged his church with new energy, he has done so by infusing the letter of his Word with new power and given his messengers greater acuity in finding its meaning and applying it to the problems that confront them. The church lives from the presence of its Lord, but the Lord who reveals himself to us still does so most movingly when he interprets the Scripture for us. Our attempts to arrive at Scriptural meanings must be seen in this light. Recent writings on the subject of forgiveness demonstrate rather clearly the need for some precision in our efforts to arrive at the meaning of the Biblical words on forgiveness. To understand and apply these words correctly to our day demands the most open sharing of insights and the most humble desire to find God's will in the written word as his community of grace interprets it. Although we must always begin with the Biblical affirmations, sound method demands that we engage in dialogue with the Biblical writers. With all that has been written on forgiveness, it is somewhat striking that no one has heretofore assembled the Biblical evidence on the meaning of forgiveness.[3]

Secondly, there is the crisis that confronts the church as it is rapidly recognizing itself as a minority group in the world and in danger of erosion from within and corrosion from without. Thanks to the ecumenical movement, in the past fifty years the nature of the church has been subjected to intense scrutiny. What a flood of monographs, articles, and popular treatments this has produced! And yet the evidence that this clearer conception of the nature of the church has resulted in church renewal beyond the inauguration of certain experiments is distressingly slim.

Where is the church? What are the marks of the "true" church? Joseph Haroutunian puts it simply: "The church is where forgiving neighbors exist."[4] Can the church then ever be the church of Jesus Christ until it has learned the dynamics of Christian forgiveness? How far can the limits of forgiveness extend? Does it extend even to the enemy who appears unrepentant to us? What is the origin of forgiveness? In what way would the church be different if it were truly a forgiving community? These are quite unacademic questions in our day when the church constantly faces the option of whether to have a significant or an insignificant existence. For many will feel that our theology of forgiveness has been defined minutely enough but that Hans Hofmann has placed his finger on the sore spot when he says:

We have failed to make clear within the context of the real life of people the meaning of forgiveness and how its reality is implemented in their appraisal of themselves and their actions.[5]

Until the church rises to the challenge of correcting this failure, until its denunciation of sin is overshadowed by and subservient to its offer of forgiveness, it has not accomplished its purpose on earth. One is tempted to paraphrase Cyprian's "outside the church there is no salvation" to "inside the church there is no forgiveness."

There is also a silent condemnation that is increasingly vocalized from the helping professions. The emergence of the new psychology, which so deeply pervades all of Western thought, has pointed to a serious weakness of Christianity: it has bungled badly the problem of guilt. Psychiatrists have advanced a cumulative mass of evidence showing that guilt (imagined or real) has caused the lives of many people to be crippled to the point of ineffectiveness. Freud, with his background in Judaism, could not help being impressed by the difficulties that are caused by pointing to man's sin but denying him a viable means of expiating his sin without providing him with clear assurance that his sins have been forgiven. Ancient Hebrew religion had a clear and forceful way of helping people to experience God's forgiving nature, but modern Judaism, Roman Catholicism with the formalization of the confessional, and Protestantism with its neglect of the confessional and the relegation of absolution to the liturgy, have created an impossible situation. The preaching of standards and values in these religions without any escape from a violation of these standards is analogous to increasing pressure until finally the conveyor has to burst.

An educational psychologist says:

We now have to recognize that Protestantism has, on the whole, handled the problem of guilt very badly and that the present critical situation is a natural culmination of four centuries of bumbling, indecision and confusion on this score.[6]

One may question the credentials of a psychologist for addressing himself to this problem, but there is no questioning the fact that psychiatry has from the outset seen it as part of its role to be a father confessor. Freud put it down clearly when he acknowledged that psychoanalysis looks as if the analyst aims at playing the part of a worldly father confessor. The great difference, Freud maintained, is "that we want to hear from our patient not only what he knows and conceals from other people, but also what he does *not* know."[7] The same opinion is expressed by Freud in his early writings and occurs also in other literature.[8]

Even if we allow for the possibility that Freud was searching for a metaphor to explain the nature of his new therapeutic method and that he was only half in earnest when he compared himself with a father confessor, we cannot deny that many people have experienced a release from guilt on the psychiatrist's couch, a release that the church did not provide. This has caused the discussion of sin, guilt, and forgiveness to arise with such urgency in the recent past.

One is tempted, in the presence of evidence of freedom from guilt in the clinic, to question the theology on which such experiences are based. It is a comparatively simple task to show the theological inadequacies of release from guilt in secular contexts. Nevertheless, we should remind ourselves that the joy of forgiveness of sins was an essential part of the life of the early church, and there is no reason to substitute a joyless orthodoxy for what the gospel offers us. Perhaps the new form of the behavioral sciences was sent to us as a reminder that God does not always get the response he wishes from those who confess him, and must then turn to other instruments who serve him unknowingly. Given such a situation, we face the task of scrutinizing, evaluating, and using that which can further the accomplishment of the church's mission.

The confluence of all these factors compels us to examine again the dynamics of Christian forgiveness. By "dynamics" is meant not only the process through which forgiveness is realized but also the power that lies behind forgiveness, enabling it to become a part of human experience. The question will be pressed: In what ways does Biblical religion not only teach that God is a forgiving God but also provide us with channels, methods, or procedures that point the way for the realization of forgiveness in human relationships? The present manuscript was completed prior to the publication of J. G. Emerson's *The Dynamics of Forgiveness.* He refers to context and instrumentation of forgiveness. Our treatments supplement each other, since my concern is with a more intimate acquaintance with the historical context of forgiveness in the Old and New Testaments.

A number of methods are available to anyone studying this subject. One can take a purely historical approach, describing what he sees in the historical material. He can take a comparative approach, at each point comparing what he thinks he sees in the Biblical material with what he sees in psychiatry. The approach that is here taken

makes certain references to psychiatric and psychological
literature without professing to canvass all the schools of
psychiatry and thus does not profess to offer an exposition
of "What Psychiatry Says About Forgiveness." Such a
study in itself could be quite helpful but outside our
province.

Our concern is to study the Biblical materials, allowing
psychological insights to take their place along with other
factors in the exegetical procedure. The recognition given
to the psychological dimension of exegesis by men like
Schleiermacher, Wilhelm Dilthey, and Frederik Torm
opens the way for such an approach. Whether one "psy-
chologizes" the Scriptures in using this approach the
reader should feel free to judge. To be sure, in doing so he
must remember that completely objective exegesis is impossible. This does not mean that sound interpretive principles can be discarded from the outset, but it does mean
that subjective factors are always affecting our interpretation more or less consciously.

There continue to be a few striking instances where
the church as a fellowship lives as a forgiving community.
Yet a great distance lies before us in even approaching the
aim of Christian forgiveness: that we forgive as God has
forgiven us.

Part One
FORGIVENESS
IN THE OLD TESTAMENT

CHAPTER I

Motive and Need for Forgiveness

The theme of forgiveness is surprisingly prominent in the Old Testament. Forgiveness is often understood as an act that emerges out of the nature of God himself and is not in the first instance a concession to human weakness. What the writers of the Old Testament understood by forgiveness becomes clear as the usage of the exact word and the auxiliary metaphors are traced in detail. In this way the richness of the imagery allows us to see the splendor and variety of the Hebrew concept of forgiveness. Relating it to other ideas such as redemption and salvation can best be done by tracing it in its historical dimension. Finally, the last part of this section looks at the psychological processes involved in forgiveness. What happened to Hebrew man as he experienced God's forgiveness? What was expected of him by way of antecedent conditions and subsequent response?

A MOTIVE FOR FORGIVENESS: THE NATURE OF GOD

Marcion was right in seeing a significant difference between the Old and the New Covenants. The church judged to be wrong his conclusion that the difference could best be reconciled by positing a God of wrath in the Old Testament and a God of love in the New.

We have clear and abundant evidence that the Old Testament portrait of God already includes his forgiving nature. This conception was not equally clearly expressed by all the writers, but a survey of the literature shows that it is not ancillary to Old Testament literature. In an analysis of this material, the historical sequence of the literature provides a convenient framework for looking at it.[1] There was obviously some development in the Israelite understanding of forgiveness, although we no longer assume that the more recent is the more valuable.

According to the Hebrew writers, God first appears as a forgiving God at the time of the establishment of the covenant with the whole people at Sinai. Prior to that, Noah, Abraham, and Lot had been spared God's acts of judgment because they were righteous. Before the Flood, forgiveness apparently did not figure prominently for the Hebrew writers. The increase of sin could result in only one course of action: the destruction of the sinner. Even though the sins of Abraham are portrayed as a breach of the newly established covenant, no explicit reference is made to forgiveness prior to the ratification of the covenant on Mt. Sinai.

The incident that prompts the mention of forgiveness is recorded in some detail in Ex., chs. 32 to 34. At the very time when God was making known the terms of the covenant to Moses, the people of Israel were committing idolatrous acts of infidelity. Moses, deeply distraught by this infidelity, intercedes on behalf of the people, offering to make atonement for their sin (ch. 32:30). In Hebrew historical material this approach to God first mentions forgiveness when the following is attributed to Moses:

But now, if thou wilt forgive their sin—and if not, blot me, I
pray thee, out of thy book which thou hast written. (V. 32.)

The response to this initial plea is that God will punish
the sin or "visit their sin upon them" (v. 34). Also, apparently there is the possibility that God will desert his
people in the same way that they have deserted him, for
he says that he will send an angel with them, "but I will
not go up among you, lest I consume you in the way, for
you are a stiff-necked people" (chs. 32:9; 33:5). As a result, however, of Moses' intercession, God's true nature is
revealed, the covenant is renewed, and as a part of this
renewal we discover what God is like:

The Lord! the Lord! a God compassionate and gracious, slow
to anger, rich in steadfast kindness, extending kindness to the
thousandth generation, forgiving iniquity, transgression, and
sin; yet He does not remit all punishment, but visits the iniquity of fathers upon children and children's children, upon
the third and fourth generations. (Ch. 34:6–7, *The Torah:
The Five Books of Moses;* The Jewish Publication Society of
America, 1962.)

On the basis of this revelation of God's nature, Moses
pleads:

Go in the midst of us, although it is a stiff-necked people; and
pardon our iniquity and sin, and take us for thy inheritance.
(V. 9.)

Here it is evident that the Hebrews based their faith in
forgiveness on the forgiving nature of God. Some examples
occur elsewhere in the Old Testament as well.

Deutero-Isaiah sees the greatness of God precisely in
the fact that God does forgive. He calls the people to:

> Seek the Lord while he may be found,
> > call upon him while he is near;
> let the wicked forsake his way,
> > and the unrighteous man his thoughts;
> let him return to the Lord, that he may have
> > mercy on him,
> and to our God, for he will abundantly pardon.
>
> > > (Isa. 55:6 f.)

The psalm writer also gives expression to his faith in a forgiving God. In Ps.86, where the writer especially cries for help, he bases his appeal upon the fact that the Lord is his God and that he is "good and forgiving" (v. 5). Thus he appeals to Yahweh's manner of dealing with his people as it has been proclaimed in Israel from earliest times (Ex. 20:6; 34:6; Num. 14:18; Ps. 103:8).[2]

Psalm 99 recounts the dealings of God with Moses and Aaron and Samuel, and while extolling the holiness of God also mentions that Yahweh answered them,

> Thou wast a forgiving God to them,
> but an avenger of their wrongdoings.
>
> > (V. 8.)

The Hebrew word used here (*nasa'*) generally means to remove or take away.[3]

One description of God's forgiving nature has created difficulties for interpreters. The psalm writer in a moment of anguish asks:

> If thou, O Lord, shouldst mark iniquities,
> > Lord, who could stand?
> But there is forgiveness with thee,
> > that thou mayest be feared.
>
> > > (Ps. 130:3–4.)

What is the relationship between honoring or fearing God and forgiveness? Does this verse mean that through forgiveness the number of those who fear God is increased? Does it mean that forgiveness brings honor and respect into being? It is probably best to take the verse as evidence for the Hebrew conception that forgiveness and honor or respect are intimately related. Forgiveness does not mean loss of face any more than it implies condoning of sins.[4]

In view of the later efforts to find motives of forgiveness elsewhere, it may be observed that forgiveness is seen by the writers of the Old Testament as an essential aspect of God's nature.[5] Most often this side of God's character is expressed together with his "visiting the iniquity of the fathers," i.e., forgiveness does not indicate that God loses his sense of value.

Forgiveness seen as an attribute of God also means that the motive of God's forgiveness is not primarily the weakness of man. It used to be asserted that forgiveness is a uniquely Biblical concept.[6] The discovery and publication of many Egyptian and Babylonian penitential psalms, however, make such a position untenable. That a different conception of sin and forgiveness is found in these cultures can be demonstrated, but that is quite a different matter from stating that forgiveness is unique to the Jewish-Christian faith.[7]

In Walther Eichrodt's discussion of forgiveness he lists three motives that may serve to summarize our discussion: There is first the loving-kindness (*hesed*) that led Yahweh to establish the covenant and that can also be relied upon to keep that covenant. "To this *hesed Yahweh*, which is dependable in every circumstance, belongs also forgiveness of transgressions."[8] God retains his freedom to punish or forgive, but his honor would be lessened if he did not forgive his people their sins.

According to Eichrodt, forgiveness is not only motivated by God's specific dealings with Israel but also by a general conception of God's tendency to be indulgent and forgiving (*"Gottes Geneigtheit zur Nachsicht und Verzeihung"*).[9] To be sure, there exists a considerable tension between this motive and the appeal to human responsibility so evident in the prophets. The psalms would seem to stress the one side, and Eichrodt concludes:

The prominence given by the Psalmist to the forgiveness of sins (based on God's inscrutable mercy and so clearly seen in Israel's history) does not permit us to see the fact that man is human as a new motive of forgiveness. It only highlights the totality of the divine father love, which stoops to such a poor creature.[10]

The deepest motive of divine forgiveness Eichrodt sees in the assertions about God's glory and his love. God deals with Israel according to a purpose he has in mind, and this purpose cannot be frustrated by their unfaithfulness.

The prophets, especially, compared God's faithfulness with man's unfaithfulness, stressed God's zeal or jealousy (*qānā'*), and made frequent reference to "the sake of his holy name" and his determination that "ye will know that I am Yahweh your God." God's consistent and dependable nature would be denied if he allowed man's unfaithfulness to deflect him from his purpose. It is his purpose to be vindicated before the eyes of the whole world that they may see that he is creator and helper of all.

Because he is helper, he cannot abandon his people in distress and transgression. As Eichrodt has noted, the fact that God does not abandon his covenant people marks the triumph of his love.[11] The generosity of the revelation of love which, by keeping the covenant in force despite man's unfaithfulness, manifests itself as a forgiving power, moreover reveals its marvelous power in that a new community is created in which both great and small experience forgiveness as an inner renewal of intimate loving fellowship with the divine Lord.[12]

THE NECESSITY FOR FORGIVENESS: SIN

Various authors have testified to the fact that in the discussion between religion and psychiatry the question of sin is the most urgent subject. Paul Tillich has recently acknowledged that the term "sin" has fallen into disrepute and that he, along with other theologians, has shied away from it because it is subject to so many misinterpretations. Yet he also recognizes that it has a strange quality of always coming back. "You cannot get rid of it. It is as insistent as it is ugly."[13]

O. Hobart Mowrer has insisted that the psychologists would do well to reckon with sin as a category.[14] Without a discussion of whether the term itself is useful to either theologians or psychologists, it must be granted that both disciplines deal with certain norms, both have their concepts of what constitutes healthy behavior, and such terms as "deviant" and "perverse" used in psychiatric theory lend support to the thesis that we have here an overlapping area that merits exploration. This is especially true if the principal problem in the tension between psychology and Christianity is the question of sin.[15] It is necessary, however, to look at the Biblical conception of sin again, for it is possible that neither the theologians who are inclined to reject the term because of its distortions, nor the psychologists who pay lip service to the term, actually express the profound reality of sin as the Old Testament sees it. Furthermore, forgiveness can be adequately understood only as we see that which is forgiven. It may not be incidental that the emphasis in Biblical literature is on forgiving sins and not people, although the two cannot really be separated.

Since the Israelites were a primitive people (by this I mean unsophisticated, prelogical, living next to nature), it is not surprising to see that for them the good action is generally the normal action. Such an act would also succeed or prosper. Actions that are not normal, or those which are only partly so, are considered sin. Sin is the opposite of rightness (or righteousness), and, properly speaking, the sinful act is not an act at all but merely a caricature. Since sin is a negative, it follows that a soul that is sinful throughout is dissolved and decayed. As Pedersen puts it:

The sinner lacks the firm center of action; his soul is not a pure and firm organism, but full of inner strife, a dissolved mass. Therefore it staggers about aimlessly, like one intoxicated. The soul of the sinner lacks firmness and strength, therefore falsehood is its characteristic feature.[16]

The Hebrew conception of falsehood is well expressed in Ps. 12:2, which describes the liar as speaking with a "double heart." As H. J. Kraus notes:

With keen psychological insight the Psalmist recognizes that the lying and flattering words of the sinner originate in a divided, discrepant heart.[17]

Falsehood for the Hebrew, then, is the same as a splitting of the soul, to act against wholeness.[18] Falsehood is determined against that which Yahweh has revealed, and to act against Yahweh's will is to bring about chaos, con-

fusion, and sickness. The classic narrative about the entry
of sin into the world recorded in Gen., ch. 3, asserts that all
troubles in human life have their cause in the one trouble
of man's ruptured relationship with God. "Gen. ch. 3
asserts that all sorrow comes from sin."[19] Given the most
ideal environment and almost unlimited freedom, man
denied God the one thing he asked for: obedience. In
doing so, he lost the openness of meeting his fellowman,
bartering it for shame. He lost his joy of encountering God,
receiving for it fear.

Apart from this narrative dealing with the etiology of
sin, the rest of the Old Testament sees sin as

the dissolution of the soul, an infringement upon its integrity
and its firmness. It is also described as hardness and stiffness,
for the normal soul is pliable and yielding, fit to subject itself
to a totality with others.[20]

What sin does to the self is described by Bultmann thus:

To be innerly divided, or not to be at one with one's self, is the
essence of human existence under sin.[21]

The three most common words used for sin in the Old
Testament are *ht'*, *awōn* and *pesha'*. The first characterizes
sin as failure to meet a standard or to arrive at a goal or to
miss an aim. The second sees sin primarily as an irregular,
"crooked," action, a deviation from normal behavior patterns. The third sees sin primarily as an infringement upon
a psychic totality. This breadth in the Hebrew concept of
sin stands in contrast to the view that sees sin primarily as
external behavior or primarily as attitude.

The basic root, *ht'*, is used over two hundred times and
means primarily to "miss the mark." It is used of a runner
who gets off the track because of haste and consequently

does not reach his destination (Prov. 19:2). In Prov. 8:36 it is used as an opposite to the word "find." It assumes that man has purpose and goal, and unless he can find that purpose he can only wander aimlessly.

The word *awōn* occurs especially frequently in the prophets. Koehler-Baumgartner indicate that it occurs some 231 times (Ezek., forty-four times; Ps., twenty-nine times; Isa., twenty-five times; Jer., twenty-four times; Lev., eighteen times; Num., twelve times; Hos., eleven times). Its basic meaning is to act crookedly or wrongly, and according to Koehler-Baumgartner, it occurs in three different senses: (*a*) conscious or intentional transgression (fifty-five times); (*b*) guilt (159 times; see especially Isa. 6:7 where it occurs alongside of *ht'*); and (*c*) punishment for guilt or transgression (seven times).

The root, *pesha'*, occurring about 150 times, implies a more definite volitional aspect. Its basic meaning is to "rise up against someone." Thus one may lose his way by error, but to rebel against someone involves a rather clear and forceful use of the will. According to E. König, this word could best be translated as "carrying out a rebellion."[22] N. Snaith also emphasizes this aspect of sin when he says: "Sin is not transgression of law but personal revolt."[23] All sin is revolt and disobedience against Yahweh.[24] Since the covenant is central for Hebrew religious thought and is that which "upholds all life," it can be said that "the breach of the covenant is the kernel of sin."[25]

The covenant, however, is given to more than one man, and through it a people came into being. Therefore, a breaking of the covenant is most often seen as an action that is related to the fellow covenant member. This leads Pedersen to describe a sinful act as an act "through which a community is dissolved."[26] The action leads to a breach of peace. What is involved is not only the failure to meet one's own obligations as a member of the covenant community but also a progressive spreading of the disease of one soul to the psychic whole, for such a breach already means that "one's own soul is diseased."

The soul only exists as a link in an organism with which it is intimately interwoven; the breach of peace is a result of the soul misjudging this reality and acting as if it were isolated, something apart. Such an act is called violence, *hāmās, shōdh,* or encroachment, *'ōshek;* it is only a delusion, not a real action, because it does not proceed from a healthy soul, acting as a link in its totality, but from a soul living in an imaginary, exceptional position, as an isolated individual, one that does not act according to the law of totality.[27]

Sin, then, has its origin in a soul that is already dissolved and spreads dissolution around to its environment. The seriousness of sin is determined by the relationship that the action has to the acting soul. Is it peripheral or central to the will of that soul? The seriousness of an act is not judged by its consequences or its inherent nature but by the degree to which it emanates from the center of one's existence.

In summary, sin is seen in the Old Testament as a state of opposition against God. It is assumed that it is God's prerogative to order the conditions of man's life, whether it be in the primal garden or under the covenant. But for some inexplicable reason man pits his will against his Maker's, thinking he can work out his own destiny through knowledge. Sin, at its core, is pitting oneself against God and the resultant breaking of relationships with the fellowman, and the disease that comes upon man himself can be seen as both cause and result of the basic insubordination to God.[28]

CHAPTER II

The Nature of Forgiveness

THE USAGE OF THE WORD "FORGIVE" (*Salach*)

Preexilic Historical Writings

J. J. Stamm has noted that when we look primarily at the terms and images used to describe forgiveness in the preexilic historical narratives, we are struck by the fact that forgiveness is more often denied or only partially granted than clearly granted.[1]

As an example of such a statement he cites Josh. 24:19:

> But Joshua said to the people, "You cannot serve the Lord; for he is a holy God; he is a jealous God; he will not forgive your transgressions or your sins."

Likewise, the angel whom God sends before his people deserves their attention and should not be resisted, "for he will not pardon your transgression; for my name is in him" (Ex. 23:21). Similarly in ch. 32:32 ff., forgiveness is not granted in a perfunctory way; indeed, it appears to have been rejected by Yahweh, for he says: "Whoever has

sinned against me, him will I blot out of my book" (v. 33).
The wrath of God will, in its own time, express itself in a
visitation from him as a direct consequence of their sin
(v. 34).

Another pathetic instance in which forgiveness is not
granted is the case of Saul. Saul had been told not to spare
any of the Amalekites, but he declined to carry out the
will of God, sparing Agag the king and also the best of
the animals. In his explanation of his action to Samuel we
have the classic aspects of sin and rebellion portrayed also
in Gen., ch. 3: the blame is deflected, an attempt is made
to justify the action by offering the spoils to God, and
when all these efforts fail, a halfhearted show of repentance is displayed. Whatever may be the reason, his request
for pardon (I Sam. 15:25) is denied, and Saul is rejected
as head of the kingdom. His verdict has been pronounced
even though he does not begin to serve his sentence immediately. There is some sin that is too grievous for expiation
—or at least there is an attitude toward it that as it persists
makes expiation impossible (I Sam. 3:14). That God manifests his acceptance through receiving an offering is plain
from a number of passages (Gen. 4:4–5; I Sam. 6:4;
26:19).

The words "forgive," "pardon," or "remit" render the
Hebrew word *salach*. It is an abstract verb whose original
locus, meaning, and history prior to its appearance in the
Old Testament are not known. Possibly it had its origin in
the Accadian *salāhu*, which means "to sprinkle." In secular
context it appears in medical texts to describe sprinkling
someone with water, oil, or other therapeutic liquids. In
cultic connections it is often related to sacrifice. It is not
clear whether the sprinkling is itself a sacrifice or only a
preparation for sacrifice. The fact that the Old Testament

writers often relate forgiveness to cleansing would argue for connecting the original meaning of forgiveness with cleansing, as appears to have been the case in Accadian.[2]

The Preexilic Prophets

The oldest occurrence of the word "forgive" is found in Amos 7:2. Here it appears in the context of the first of the five visions of Amos, the vision of the locusts. After the destruction they create, Amos pleads:

> O Lord God, forgive, I beseech thee!
> How can Jacob stand?
> He is so small!
>
> (V. 2.)

Yahweh answers his prayer and Amos says that He repented concerning this: " 'It shall not be,' said the Lord" (v. 3). It appears that God here changes his mind, since he does not carry through an intended punishment. What is of interest in this passage is that Amos sees himself in the role of an intercessor, which is all the more striking if his rejection of the priesthood and the cultus is as absolute as certain scholars have asserted.[3] Much has been written about the prophets' rejection of the cultus, and the impressive list of names given by Hentschke on both sides of this controversy makes it clear that this issue has not yet been resolved. Yet a reading of the total literary material without a predetermined bias leads to agreement with the verdict of Markus Barth:

The cheap contrast between ethical-prophetical and ceremonial-priestly teachings and writings is ripe for a final revision, or better, for burial without honour.[4]

Amos sees the grace as well as the punishment of God and his appeal is based upon the hope that

> it may be that the Lord, the God of hosts,
> will be gracious to the remnant of Joseph.
> (Ch. 5:15.)

Another occurrence of the word "forgive" is found in II Kings, ch. 5, in an intriguing context. Naaman the Syrian had been healed of his leprosy and had returned to give the prophet Elisha a gift. When this gift was refused, Naaman vowed that he would worship only the God of Israel and desired to take home some earth for that purpose. As a subordinate of the king of Syria, he is aware that occasions will arise when he will accompany the king into the house of Rimmon to worship there. Thus he requests:

> In this matter may the Lord pardon your servant: when my master goes into the house of Rimmon to worship there, leaning on my arm, and I bow myself in the house of Rimmon, when I bow myself in the house of Rimmon, the Lord pardon your servant in this matter. (II Kings 5:18.)

Some have seen here a case in which pardon is granted prior to the act, for the prophet replies: "Go in peace" (v. 19). Ludwig Köhler writes,

> Here *salach* is forbearance, not real forgiveness, since there is no remorse and no resolution to abandon the thing regretted.

Elisha merely encourages him to expect a certain degree of indulgence on the part of Yahweh.[5] If so, then we have here another instance in which the preexilic literature does not assure forgiveness but only expresses a hope for it.

The Pentateuch

The two occurrences of the term "forgive" in the older layers of the Pentateuch are in prayers, both uttered by Moses. Mention has already been made of the prayer of

Moses at the time of the apostasy of the people of Israel at Mt. Sinai (Ex. 34:9), which concludes:

Forgive us our iniquity and transgression and make us your own possession.

Again in Num. 14:13–19, Moses intercedes for the people when they grumble at the report of the spies. Moses appeals to the honor of God and notes that if the whole people are destroyed, it will be noised abroad that God was unable to bring his people into the Promised Land, and the Egyptians will hear of it.

He appeals to God's original disclosure of himself as being a forgiving God (ch. 14:18) and then pleads:

Pardon the iniquity of this people, I pray thee, according to the greatness of thy steadfast love, and according as thou hast forgiven this people, from Egypt even until now. (V. 19.)

This is apparently the first instance in which the intercession is rewarded with the explicit granting of pardon when the Lord says: "I have pardoned, according to your word" (v. 20).

Jeremiah

In The Book of Jeremiah forgiveness is mentioned several times. In the same way that the preexilic historical material seems to underline the fact that forgiveness does not automatically occur, Jeremiah highlights the sins of Israel when God asks through him:

> How can I pardon you?
>   Your children have forsaken me,
>   and have sworn by those who are no gods.
> When I fed them to the full,
>   they committed adultery
>   and trooped to the houses of harlots.

They were well-fed lusty stallions,
　　each, neighing for his neighbor's wife.
Shall I not punish them for these things?
　　　　　　　　　says the Lord;
　　and shall I not avenge myself
　　on a nation such as this?

(Ch. 5:7–9.)

In the beginning of ch. 5, Jeremiah has called his fellow Israelites to join in a search for just one man "who does justice and seeks truth" (v. 1), but their search has revealed no one. The question is then raised: "How can I pardon?" and it is not to be taken in an apodictic sense but rather as a rhetorical question.[6] Given this debased state and this unrepentant attitude, what can the possible motive for forgiveness be? In the case of Sodom and Gomorrah (Gen. 18:32), Abraham courageously interceded on behalf of the righteous ones, going as low as ten. Here in Jeremiah we seem to have an implication that if there is even one who is righteous, God will spare the city.[7]

That God has not given up is clear from Jer. 36:3, where Yahweh urges the prophet to write down these words because

it may be that the house of Judah will hear all the evil which I intend to do to them, so that everyone may turn from his evil way, and that I may forgive their iniquity and their sin.

Here forgiveness is seen as the motive behind the writing of the prophet so that the people may be brought to their senses, that the threats of punishment from Yahweh may cause them to change their behavior and thus avert the punishment of God. According to this view, forgiveness is a process that takes place within the world and depends upon human attitudes and behavior.[8]

In addition to this, Jeremiah sees forgiveness as a reality that is fully attainable only in the New Age. In that classic passage, looking forward to the new covenant, forgiveness of sins is the presupposition of the new covenant. In that day the Lord will forgive their iniquity and remember their sin no more (ch. 31:34). In the same way, ch. 33:8 promises that in the last day

I will cleanse them from all the guilt of their sin against me, and I will forgive all the guilt of their sin and rebellion against me.

The day will even come when

iniquity shall be sought in Israel, and there shall be none; and sin in Judah, and none shall be found; for I will pardon those whom I leave as a remnant (ch. 50:20).

Isaiah 55:6 f., which also sets the forgiveness of sins in an eschatological future, is probably somewhat older than the Jeremiah references. The phrases "while he may be found" and "while he is near" seem to suggest a day in the future when this will not be the case. The words "he will abundantly pardon" (ch. 55:7) indicate that it is Yahweh's nature to forgive. According to this passage, forgiveness is not dependent upon man's attitude, for it is predicated by the nature of God, and thus is antecedent to every human accomplishment. Man is invited to lay hold upon God's salvation through the changing of his ways.[9] It is not characteristic for this prophet to join his promises of forgiveness with demands upon Israel.[10] In all the eschatological passages, forgiveness is seen not as a prerequisite but as a consequence of the coming of the Kingdom.

Deuteronomic Writings

The Deuteronomic writings provide one occurrence of the word "forgive" in the book of Deuteronomy in a context where the danger of merely listening to the reading of the words of the covenant is stressed. The one who congratulates himself as he hears the words of the covenant read and is secure in the stubbornness of his heart will bring God's sweeping broom upon the total people.

> The Lord would not pardon him, but rather the anger of the Lord and his jealousy would smoke against that man, and the curses written in this book would settle upon him, and the Lord would blot out his name from under heaven. (Deut. 29:20; v. 19 in Hebrew.)

By contrast, the word "forgive" occurs five times in the Deuteronomic prayer of dedication of the Temple (I Kings 8:14–66; II Chron. 6:3–42). It first appears as a part of the petition that God will hear their prayer and that as he hears he may forgive (I Kings 8:30; II Chron. 6:21), and then in consecutive petitions: the first dealing with defeat from an enemy (I Kings 8:34; II Chron. 6:24 f.); the second dealing with drought (I Kings 8:36; II Chron. 6:26 f.); the third dealing with famine, pestilence, etc., or any other plague (I Kings 8:37; II Chron. 6:28–31); and finally, a fourth, when they are led into captivity because of their sin, and they cry to God for forgiveness that he may grant it (I Kings 8:50; II Chron. 6:39). In each of these passages except the first, sin and punishment are combined, and forgiveness is identified with the cessation of God's act of punishment. Sin's presence evokes the punitive hand of God as manifested in plagues, captivity, or drought. Thus forgiveness means not only removal of the sin but also of its consequences, the calamity that is understood as punishment. J. J. Stamm has noted, "Forgiveness is here always joined to an external confirmation."[11] And yet I Kings 8:50 is remarkable in that the answer to the prayer does not assume that with forgiveness will also come a return from exile but, rather, that the captors will have compassion on them.

Two features stand out in these Deuteronomic passages: (1) Answer to prayer and forgiveness are intimately joined together (I Kings 8:27–30: "When thou hearest, forgive," v. 30). This union between hearing prayer and forgiveness is common in Biblical literature and may be related to the Biblical conception of "hearing." God hears prayer when he gives us what we need most: forgiveness.[12] (2) For the most part, forgiveness is here seen as the removal of the punishment.

Another passage, II Kings 24:1–4, assumes the same identification but states that God does not grant pardon but allows the sins of the previous generation to continue to work their evil course. The historical writer interprets the events and says:

Surely this came upon Judah at the command of the Lord, . . . for the sins of Manasseh, according to all that he had done, . . . and the Lord would not pardon. (Vs. 3–4.)

Thus, according to this historian, if forgiveness had been forthcoming, the present crisis of the people would have been mitigated.

Priestly Material

In the Priestly material the experience of forgiveness is intimately related to atonement and sacrifice. Forgiveness comes as atonement is made through sacrifice for a transgression. Thus forgiveness comes through the guilt offering alone (Lev. 4:20,26,31,35; 5:6,13) or through a guilt offering together with a burnt offering (chs. 5:16; 17:6; 19:22). Yahweh does forgive even without a sacrifice in the case where a woman makes a vow that cannot stand because of the disapproval of her father (Num. 30:5), or husband (vs. 8,12). Since forgiveness here is a consequence of God's consideration of purely external factors, and her attitude is not brought into the picture at all, it is possible that *salach* here means simply to be indulgent or understanding.[13]

Postexilic Material

Postexilic passages that mention forgiveness include Lam. 3:42, in which the prophet admonishes his people:

> Let us test and examine our ways,
>   and return to the Lord!
> Let us lift up our hearts and hands to
>   God in heaven:
> "We have transgressed and rebelled,
>   and thou hast not forgiven.
> Thou hast wrapped thyself with anger and pursued us,
>   slaying without pity;
> thou hast wrapped thyself with a cloud
>   so that no prayer can pass through."
>
> (Vs. 40–44.)

Again the dilemma of the present is seen as a result of past misdeeds, and the nonforgiveness of sins is seen as an important factor in their present plight.

The verb "forgive" (*salach*) occurs only in two psalms, both of which are postexilic. In Ps. 25 we meet a person who has obvious concern about the sins of his youth (v. 7) and prays that God will not remember them. Three times in this short psalm he asks for forgiveness (vs. 7, 11, 18), although the verb *salach* occurs only once (v. 11). The verb *nasa'* appears in v. 18. The first petition is based on God's steadfast love (*hesed*), the second is based on God's name (v. 11), and the third is based on the loneliness, affliction, troubles, and distresses of the writer (v. 18). The writer obviously labors under an acute sense of guilt, which is explicitly expressed in v. 11 when he says: "Pardon my guilt, for it is great."

Psalm 103:3 is written in a quite different mood. Likewise postexilic, it seems to reverberate with joy and praise because of the certainty that forgiveness has been granted and with it the healing of all diseases (v. 3). Since sickness is often seen as a result of transgression in the Old Testament, it is not surprising to find forgiveness and healing related here.[14] Healing serves as the evidence of forgiveness.

The verb *salach* finally occurs in the prayer of Daniel recorded in Dan. 9:4–19. Verse 9 has described forgiveness as belonging to God, and his prayer ends with the petition: "O Lord, hear; O Lord, forgive" (v. 19). Throughout the prayer one detects a deep sense of sin, and Daniel sees himself as a part of a sinning people.[15] Because of his sins and those of the fathers, Jerusalem and God's people have become a mockery (v. 16). Even the exile, God's severest judgment against them, did not result in repentance. All that remains now is the hope that God will forgive purely for his own name's sake, on the grounds of his great mercy. There is no longer any hope in man's ability to return.

The later literature also uses the adjectival form *slh*, "forgiving" or "being ready to forgive" (Ps. 86:5), and the substantive, "forgiveness" (singular and plural), occurs in Ps. 130:4; Dan. 9:9; Neh. 9:17.

IMAGES BY WHICH FORGIVENESS IS PORTRAYED

In recent discussions about method in Biblical study there has been considerable focus on the propriety of the method of word study. While Biblical study has often been characterized by meticulous linguistic analysis, including etymology and meaning as decided by usage, there has also been a strong movement in the direction of studying "concepts" or relating the theological and linguistic meanings. The monumental *Theological Wordbook*, founded by Gerhard Kittel and now edited by G. Friedrich, the first volume of which is now available in English, has recently been sharply criticized by James Barr primarily on the basis of such a method.[16]

That such criticism is to some extent justified cannot be doubted. In a work of such magnitude there is bound to be inconsistency in the application of a method as well as introjection of theological bias in the conclusions. However, Barr's critique centers on the basic weakness of the method itself, and there is something to be said for this even from a perspective different from his. One limitation of the method is that focusing on a word study fails to deal with the concept where a different word is used to describe it. In the present study, therefore, the assumption is that forgiveness cannot be studied only where the precise word occurs, but must be studied also where other words occur to describe the dynamic process that is involved. The realities of Biblical religion are all too often reduced to a shallow insipidness or domesticated by settling on a favorite image to describe one aspect of the experience. Experience, certainly religious experience, cannot, however, be reduced to any facile formula, and the Biblical writers themselves can only be reduced to pat formulas by a kind of forceful seduction. A study of the nature of Biblical forgiveness must permit its richness to be conveyed by looking at the variety of images used to portray it.[17]

In addition to the abstract term "forgive," the Old Testament writers use some picture language to describe what takes place in forgiveness.[18] Most of these images are taken from the cultic realm and presuppose a conception of sin corresponding to the image used to portray forgiveness.

Carrying Off the Sin

One word picture is "to take away sin" or "guilt." The Hebrew word used is *nasa'*. Stamm has noted that in preexilic times this expression is used most often in the writings considered the "deuteronomic history book," and that it expresses not only the removal of sin by God but also the forgiveness of a transgression among men. Examples of this usage are: Ex. 10:17 (Pharaoh's request to Moses); Gen. 50:17 (Joseph's brothers); I Sam. 15:25 (Saul asks Samuel that his sins be forgiven); and I Sam. 25:28 (Abigail's request that David forgive her). The term is used of the angel of God in Ex. 23:21 (E).

Preexilic texts that describe the forgiveness of Yahweh in these terms are Hos. 14:3, which

expresses the expectation that Jahweh will carry away the trespass and remove it to such an extent that it will no longer harm the guilty one (cf. Ex. 32:32; 34:7; Isa. 33:24; Num. 14:18; Josh. 24:19).[19]

Postexilic occurrences include Ps. 25:18; 32:1, 5; 85:3; Micah 7:18; and Job 7:21. The verb is already used absolutely in Hos. 1:6 (i.e., without object), thus indicating its firm place in the literature.

In preexilic time the expression "to take away sin" seems to be confined primarily to the narrative material. The only exceptions appear to be Hos. 1:6 and 14:2. Most often it is found in direct address. Perhaps the underlying assumption is that sin is a load that a person takes upon himself and as such has to be removed. At times the expression "bear sin" or "iniquity" occurs in a cultic context (Lev. 20:20; 24:15; Num. 9:13; 18:22; Ezek. 23:49). Isaiah 53:12 would seem to thus view sin when it describes the servant in the words: "He bore the sin of many."

Likewise, Lev. 16:22 tells us that after Aaron has laid both his hands upon the head of the goat and confessed over him all the iniquities of the people of Israel, and all their transgressions, and all their sins, that he shall put them upon the head of the goat, and send him away into the wilderness.

The goat shall bear all their iniquities upon him to a solitary land; and he shall let the goat go in the wilderness.

It is possible that this originated in a primitive magical rite, and Isaiah's description (ch. 53:12) is a development of this magical rite. According to it, the guiltless would take the sin upon himself, thus bearing it or carrying it away. The image of the scapegoat portrays concretely what the term "forgiveness" portrays abstractly. In the life of the prophet this bearing of the punishment of Isreal becomes quite concrete (Ezek., ch. 4).

The Removal of Sin

Another expression is used to describe forgiveness in two preexilic passages: II Sam. 24:10 and ch. 12:13. In the last passage Nathan promises David that "the Lord also has put away your sin; you shall not die." The identical phrase in the Hebrew of II Sam. 24:10 is found in I Chron. 21:8, translated: "take away the iniquity of thy servant" in the RSV.

In postexilic passages this expression occurs in Job 7:21 and in Zech. 3:4. In the latter, the context would seem to suggest a possible physical source for the figure of speech. Joshua the high priest was standing before the angel of the Lord, clothed in filthy garments, and the angel commanded those standing around him, "Remove the filthy garments from him." Then the angel said to Joshua: "Behold I have taken your iniquity away from you, and I will clothe you with rich apparel" (Zech. 3:4). Although the Hebrew does not have the same verb in each case, the parallel between the two is clear. Just as dirty clothes are removed from the high priest, so also his sins are removed from him. Forgiveness is seen here primarily as cleansing and renewal.

Covering Sin

Several times the term "to cover" sin is used. In Neh. 4:5 reference is made to "covering guilt" and sin being "blotted out." Perhaps the primary reference here is to atonement and not forgiveness. In Ps. 32:1 and 85:3 it is certainly used in that way. In Prov. 17:9 the reference is to human relations:

> He who covers an offense seeks love,
>   but he who repeats a matter alienates a friend.

A close connection between atonement and forgiveness is thus established, but it rests on a broader theology, not only on these few usages.

Sweeping Sin Away

The image of sweeping away or wiping away sins is also used several times. In Deutero-Isaiah, God is pictured in these words:

> I have swept away your transgressions like a cloud,
>   and your sins like mist.
>
> (Isa. 44:22.)

Prior to that, in the controversy of the Lord with his people he declares:

> I, I am He
>> who blots out your transgressions for my own sake,
>> and I will not remember your sins.
>
> (Ch. 43:25.)

It occurs further in Neh. 4:5; Jer. 18:23; and in several psalms. In an imprecatory psalm we read:

> May the iniquity of his fathers be remembered before the Lord,
>> and let not the sin of his mother be blotted out!
>
> (Ps. 109:14.)[20]

Other passages from The Psalms that convey this same thought are Ps. 51:9: "Hide thy face from my sins, and blot out all my iniquities," and ch. 51:1: "According to thy abundant mercy blot out my transgressions." Since the mention of blotting out transgressions is often connected with "not remembering any more," Stamm has suggested that the primary reference is to erase from a book in which the sin has been recorded. It would appear that both a legal and a cultic lustration symbol are joined here in an attempt to portray the meaning of forgiveness.

Washing Away Sin

The Reformers already noted that for the Christian understanding of forgiveness no psalm was richer in content than Ps. 51. None so clearly states that only God can remove the wall that separates man from him. All that man can do is to acknowledge his guilt and ask for forgiveness. Here we have the image of bleaching or purging of sin. Both in v. 2 and in v. 7 the image of washing is used:

> Wash me thoroughly from my iniquity,
>> and cleanse me from my sin!

Later in v. 7:

> Purge me with hyssop, and I shall be clean;
> wash me, and I shall be whiter than snow.

It is possible that the background of these lines is some ritual bath of cleansing in which the participant was assured forgiveness.

The above survey of the use of terms denoting forgiveness gives some evidence of the richness of the Old Testament conception of forgiveness. We have noted that the origin of many of these images is vague and incomprehensible to the modern man. Yet there are aspects of this view that still speak with striking relevance to human need, and these deserve further attention. To focus these more sharply, the total concept of forgiveness is viewed now in historical and theological perspective. The practical experience of sinners in the Old Testament will be looked at together with the theoretical views of forgiveness that have already been observed.

Chapter III

The Experience of Forgiveness

FORGIVENESS IN THEOLOGICAL AND HISTORICAL PERSPECTIVE

Preexilic Historical Writings

In II Sam. 24:10, David, compelled by his conscience, confesses that he committed a sin in taking a census of the people and asks for forgiveness. This is granted him in part, as is evidenced by the fact that he is allowed to choose one of three punishments (vs. 13 f.). According to v. 16, however, the punishment is mitigated one further step in that Jerusalem is saved from the plague. The reason that is given is that "the Lord repented of the evil" (v. 16). The narrative in vs. 18–25 stands in contrast to this explanation, for we are told in these verses that David bought a threshing floor to build an altar for Yahweh in order to avert the plague from the people (v. 21). Consequently, some scholars feel that these two narratives have been joined together.[1] It is possible that this represents an early attempt to join forgiveness with the cultus.

The only clear realization of forgiveness in the pre-exilic historical material is II Sam., ch. 12. The prophet Nathan assures David, who had committed adultery, that "the Lord also has put away your sin; you shall not die" (v. 13). The evidence for his forgiveness is the saving of his own life, but the infant must die. The forgiveness of Yahweh is clearly expressed and is actively portrayed, but again the punishment is not removed; it is simply made less severe. Confession is clearly a presupposition of, and antecedent to, forgiveness. David recognized his sin as a result of Nathan's appeal and not through the punishment, which came later. In v. 22b we see that David saw the sickness of the child as a consequence of God's wrath. David still hopes that God's grace will come to expression in this case and the child will be saved.

We find twice in the Pentateuch a prayer of Moses for the forgiveness of the sins of the people. In both cases the prayer is answered, but it is answered especially clearly in Num. 14:20. Again we see that forgiveness expresses itself through an amelioration of the punishment from Yahweh. Instead of the announced destruction of the total people (v. 12), the punishment consists in that the generation of the people who left Egypt will not enter into the Promised Land (vs. 22–23). Numbers 14:18 and Ex. 34:6 f. seem to express the idea already that the nature of forgiveness includes punishment, but that punishment can often be made easier as a result of forgiveness. This verse seems to ground forgiveness in Yahweh's nature as experienced in history, for as Num. 14:19 puts it, ever since the deliverance from Egypt, God has forgiven his people. Both passages seem to contain a kernel that goes back to the earliest strata, J and E. Yet both are developed further. Especially the statement that God is willing to forgive and the allusion to the forgiveness that God has granted ever since the people left Egypt seem to come from the Deuteronomic material. At least, such an influence cannot be ruled out. This passage illustrates the important place that the intercession of the leader has in the experience of forgiveness.

This would seem to exhaust the preexilic texts describing the experience of forgiveness. At times the zealous nature of Yahweh is such that forgiveness is completely ruled out (Josh. 24:19; Ex. 23:31), for the petition for forgiveness is not fulfilled (Ex. 32:30–34; I Sam. 15:24 f.). Where forgiveness is granted to a greater or lesser degree (Ex. 34:6 f.; Num. 14:11 f.; II Sam. 12:13; 24:13 f.), it does not mean a total suspension of punishment but rather a mitigation of the same. Most often, forgiveness is connected with some external, recognizable evidence. It is also significant that in II Sam., chs. 12 and 24, forgiveness is preceded by confession of sin. Thus forgiveness is not received without some conditions. The assurance that forgiveness is realizable is expressed by the prophet and the man of God.

These passages do not exhaust all that the older literature has to say on forgiveness. Both the Yahwist and the Elohist already allude to the antecedents of forgiveness. Artur Weiser has observed that the view of God that comes to us from the ancient narratives in Genesis leaves considerable room for the mercy and goodness of God with respect to men who are laden with sin.[2] After the terrible consequences of divine righteousness, the primitive historian often indicates hope for the future that God will not destroy man because of the wickedness of his heart (Gen. 8:21 f.). In Gen. 4:11 f., Cain is cursed, and yet he is promised the protection of Yahweh. We find the same phenomenon in the stories of the patriarchs, in which Yahweh often does punish their sins and yet does not withdraw his favor from them. Abraham, in spite of his sin in Egypt, can return to the Promised Land (ch. 20). Jacob's guile does not result in his loss of the blessing (ch. 27:27–29); in fact, it is renewed as he returns to the Promised Land (ch. 32:25 f.). The brothers of Joseph are protected from punishment, and experience the grace of God through the forces of destiny.

Thus it would seem that the material which does not use the word forgiveness to any extent still conveys the impression that Yahweh does not always destroy the sinner but is gracious toward him. Yahweh is willing to look beyond the sins of the people, and when he does punish, this punishment is to lead them finally to the divine mercy. The older material conveys the impression that God is willing to forgive, even though this is not expressly stated.

Preexilic Prophets

Since there is a strong element of judgment in the preexilic prophets, it is not surprising that a rejection of forgiveness is at times found there. It is expressed perhaps most sharply in Isa. 22:14 in the words " 'Surely this iniquity will not be forgiven you till you die,' says the Lord God of hosts." The iniquity that will not be forgiven is the self-sufficiency and self-security on which the inhabitants of Jerusalem are depending, and the flippancy with which the people are discussing the real danger of their present situation.

Jeremiah

The sources examined thus far show us forgiveness as an object of man's prayer. Only rarely do our sources reveal forgiveness purely as a gift of Yahweh. According to

Jer. 36:3, Yahweh is ready to forgive the people their sin and guilt, but the prerequisite for it is that they will return everyone from his evil way. By contrast, ch. 31:31–34 also mentions forgiveness but does not mention man's repentance. In this latter passage the expression of forgiveness, or its result, seems to be nothing external but the possession of a new knowledge of God. Apparently Jeremiah sees forgiveness as a free gift of God that will come only in the future. Nevertheless, he admonishes the people and encourages them to achieve temporal forgiveness through repentance and conversion (ch. 36:3).

Jeremiah also has the most explicit statement questioning the validity of sacrifices and their original institution when he says:

For in the day that I brought them out of the land of Egypt, I did not speak to your fathers or command them concerning burnt offerings and sacrifices. (Ch. 7:22.)

If the ancient Israelites assumed that forgiveness could be obtained through sacrifice *and* intercession, Jeremiah certainly did not question the value of intercession. In fervent identification with his people he pleaded for forgiveness, even though he appears pessimistic about their willingness to receive it (cf. ch. 14:7 f.). Herner has noted that when Moses, Samuel, and Amos prayed for the people, they did not generally consider themselves guilty along with the people, but Jeremiah identifies himself with his people even in their sin.[3] In a moment of acute despair he prays that God will not forgive his enemies (ch. 18:23).

In the midst of Jeremiah's despair he looks forward to the time when God's covenant will be internalized and the law will be written on the tablets of the human heart (ch. 33). In this vision he sees especially clearly that forgiveness depends not upon human effort but exclusively

on the grace of God. We see in Jeremiah an emphasis on
the personal rather than on the cultic or ritualistic[4] relationships toward God.

Hosea

Hosea emphasizes greatly the acknowledgment of sin
and remorse as a prerequisite for forgiveness. As Hempel
has expressed it, Hosea's view is that "God punishes sin
and uses the punishment as an educational means to open
the door to forgiveness."[5] Repentance does not force God
to give forgiveness, because his love is given freely (Hos.
14:3). Yahweh's relationship to the sinning people is not
dependent upon human acts.

The Book of Hosea provides an unusual insight into the
ways in which the prophets sought to portray God's relation to his people. H. W. Wolff has observed that the concept of guilt and sin is conceived in an especially broad
way here. Guilt is seen by Hosea primarily as a disruption
of personal union of Israel with God, who has throughout
their history always turned toward them in love, as the
parables of the husband (ch. 2:4–22), of the father (ch.
11:1 f.), and of the physician (chs. 7:1; 14:4) show most
movingly.

From these illustrations derive a colorful variety of specific
Hoseanic expressions for sin, which should help every preacher
to prevent monotony of expression. In addition to the unusually frequent expression "to commit harlotry" or "play the
harlot" (chs. 1:2; 2:4–7; 3:3; 4:10–18; 5:3 f.; 6:10; 9:1), he
uses the terms: "no longer know Yahweh" (chs. 2:8; 5:4; 11:3);
"to forget the Lord" (chs. 2:13; 4:6; 8:14; 13:6); "to forsake
the Lord" (ch. 4:10); "pursue her lovers" instead of the Lord
(chs. 2:7,13; 11:2); "to stray from Yahweh" (ch. 7:13);
"rebel against Yahweh" (v. 13); or against the law (ch. 8:1);
they "break his covenant" (chs. 6:7; 8:1); "turn to other gods"
(ch. 3:1); they "dealt faithlessly with the Lord" (chs. 5:7; 6:7);

they are stubborn calves (ch. 4:16). There are many expressions for falseness: deal falsely (ch. 7:1); treachery (v. 3); fruit of lies (ch. 10:13); multiply falsehood (ch. 12:1), etc. The result is that Israel is without orientation, like a dove, silly and without sense (ch. 7:11). Israel is an unwise son (ch. 13:13); she staggers like a drunkard (ch. 4:11) and has consecrated herself to shame (ch. 9:10).[6]

Hosea joins such a varied description of the totality of man's alienation from God to a stress on the tenderness of God's wooing and his continued desire to win back his unfaithful spouse. The severest punishment imaginable is to be called no longer God's people and not to experience his forgiveness (ch. 1:6).[7] Both Hosea and Jeremiah encourage men to repent in order to prepare them to receive forgiveness. But forgiveness is always a free gift of God completely independent of man's actions. As Herner puts it: "Forgiveness becomes [for Hosea] purely a matter of grace."[8]

Isaiah

There are a number of occasions where the words for atonement and cleansing of sin are equivalent to forgiveness. This is especially true in the postexilic prophets, although not confined to them. Perhaps the most outstanding example is Isa. 6:7. Isaiah has become aware of his own uncleanness and confesses it, along with the uncleanness of the people with whom he dwells. Thereupon one of the seraphim flies to him, having in his hand a burning coal that has been removed from the altar. With this he touches the mouth of Isaiah and says, "Behold, this has touched your lips; your guilt is taken away, and your sin forgiven." It is apparent that this is more than simply the dedication of his lips, yet to qualify for a sacrifice it should involve some action on the part of Isaiah. Aside from his confession, there is none.

Since Isaiah's experience takes place in the Temple apart from the ministry of its priesthood, this incident throws light on the relationship between the Temple and the experience of forgiveness. Isaiah's purification comes through fire. If Isaiah's action here is an atonement sacrifice, it is striking that a heavenly creature carries it out, and it appears to have an exclusively heavenly origin. Perhaps we have here a parallel to other incidents in the Old Testament in which Yahweh himself must reconcile purely out of grace. Psalm 78:38 would offer a parallel. Isaiah, ch. 6, contains no prayer for forgiveness but only a fearful confession of guilt and the recognition that only punishment is deserved.

This would accord with Isaiah's basic position that it is not the sacrificial system itself that is wrong but the fact that the people do not allow this system to reform their lives. Thus the result is merely that the animals "trample over the Temple courts" (ch. 1:12), and hands that are stained with blood and raised in prayer cannot be accepted (v. 15). Forgiveness is achieved through repentance, for "turning" and "healing" go together (ch. 6:10); "in returning and rest you shall be saved" (ch. 30:15), and faith results in a purposeful life, for "he who believes will not be confused" (ch. 28:16). Faith is of paramount importance, for "if you will not believe, surely you will not be established" (ch. 7:9). The least that God requests is a "reasoning together" in which it is promised:

> Though your sins are like scarlet,
> they shall be as white as snow;
> though they are red like crimson,
> they shall become like wool.

> (Ch. 1:18.)[9]

Isaiah also records a writing by Hezekiah, who had been ill and been given an additional fifteen years to live. He sees in this restoration of life evidence of forgiveness, "for thou hast cast all my sins behind thy back" (ch. 38:17).

Does not the call to repentance and conversion in itself assume that God is ready to forgive the confessed and bereaved sin? Jeremiah 36:3 and Amos 3:6 and 5:14 f. seem to indicate the same. Hosea 14:1 explicitly makes this connection. The fervent plea of Isaiah (ch. 1:10–17) that the people might repent is undergirded by the conviction that the Lord alone can make their sin as white as snow (v. 18). God asks only that they be "willing and obedient" (v. 19).

Thus it would seem that the concept of forgiveness as we meet it in the preexilic prophets contains essentially the same elements that are found in the older narratives. Forgiveness includes the removal of sin, to which is related either the amelioration or the suspension of punishment. Yahweh's holiness and righteousness repeatedly denies forgiveness or allows it to be realized only in part. Nevertheless, after the judgment Yahweh reveals himself as willing and ready to forgive. Prerequisites for the experience of forgiveness appear to be recognizing the sin that was committed and turning away from it. An element not found in the earlier historical literature is the appearance of forgiveness as an eschatological event. Most important, perhaps, is the evidence that where sin is acknowledged and the purifying forgiveness of God accepted, man is commissioned and enabled for service (ch. 6).[10]

Prophets of the Exile

Among the exilic prophets we find that Ezekiel, as well as Hosea, Isaiah, and Jeremiah, visualizes the time of the future without any sin. According to Ezekiel, however, this removal of sin takes place through a cultic cleansing (Ezek. 36:25).

I will sprinkle clean water upon you, and you shall be clean from all your uncleannesses, and from all your idols I will cleanse you.

(Cf. further vs. 29 and 33.) Ezekiel perceives sin whether committed in the sanctuary (ch. 5:11) or in idolatry (chs. 20:26, 30, 31; 22:4) as pollution. Correspondingly, being freed from sin takes place not through a word of absolution but through a cleansing ritual. Since, however, it is God who performs this ceremony of cleansing, it is the equivalent of forgiveness.[11] In the future God will establish an everlasting covenant with men

that you may remember and be confounded, and never open your mouth again because of your shame, when I forgive you all that you have done, says the Lord God. (Ch. 16:63.)

Ezekiel sees the one who responds to God's call in repentance as the one who enters into life, whereas the one who does not respond will die. Life is connected with the forgiveness of sins (ch. 18:22). God has repeatedly accepted his people in spite of their sins (ch. 20:9,14,22), and in the end he will give them grace for his name's sake and accept them in grace (v. 40).

For Deutero-Isaiah, the terms "redemption" and "forgiveness" are very intimately related. He does use the term "forgive" (*salach*) in Isa. 55:7, and in two other places he uses the image of wiping away the sins (chs. 43:25; 44:22). The latter verse poetically puts it, "I have swept away your transgressions like a cloud, and your sins like mist." Here forgiveness and redemption are the two acts of Yahweh that are to move the people to conversion. Forgiveness apparently precedes redemption, and both are given as a gift of God. Neither is in merit of the people or of the individual; rather, Yahweh continually forgives his ever-sinning people in order to move them to a complete conversion. When Yahweh forgives, he does so because it is his nature (ch. 43:25), and his redemption is meant to glorify his name (ch. 44:23). One presupposition seems to be joined to the redemption that has already been achieved. Yahweh is ready to forgive after the sins of the people have been atoned through the exile. As a part of his call, the prophet hears the words spoken by the heavenly beings,

Speak to the heart of Jerusalem and cry to her that her warfare is ended, that her iniquity is pardoned, that she has received from the Lord's hand double for all her sins. (Ch. 40:1–2.)

Thus the exile is described as the double repayment for the sins of the people (cf. chs. 50:1; 54:7 f.). The past sins have been atoned, and for the present, Yahweh is ready to forgive. According to Stamm, Deutero-Isaiah sees Yahweh's redemptive working in three stages. In the beginning, the earlier sins are punished through the exile, then follows the redemption and with it, finally, the forgiveness of the sins of the present.[12]

Postexilic Prophets

The first of the postexilic prophets is Trito-Isaiah. He mentions forgiveness only once, and that in the form of a petition (Isa. 64:9). It is remarkable that a man who has such a deep knowledge of sin (cf. chs. 58; 59) would mention forgiveness only once, especially since sin seems to be for him the main factor that restrains the coming of redemption. Yet it may be that when he talks about healing (chs. 57:18; 58:8) and of redemption, he also thinks of forgiveness. This especially seems to be the case in ch. 59:20, where reference is made to coming as redeemer to those who turn from transgression. Certainly the promise in ch. 57:16 "I will not contend for ever" also includes Yahweh's willingness to forgive. In ch. 33:24, full forgiveness in the future will express itself in the fact that sickness will be extinct.[18] According to these passages, forgiveness is not a gift that makes the coming of the time of redemption possible, but one of the factors contributing to it.

In Zech. 3:4 the angel takes away the guilt of the high priest Joshua along with the symbolic act of taking away his filthy clothes. Later on, the promise is given that in a day in the future the Lord of Hosts will remove the guilt of this land in a single day (v. 9). In another vision he sees the guilt taken away to Babylon (ch. 5:5–11). In the future, the final day, the prophet looks for a time when a fountain will be opened for the house of David and the inhabitants of Jerusalem, to cleanse them from sin and uncleanness (ch. 13.1).

Not only do these prophets visualize full forgiveness in the future, but behind their call to repentance lies the obvious assumption that if they will turn to God, he will turn to them (ch. 1:3). Joel 2:13 and Mal. 3:7 also give expression to this conviction.

The Deuteronomic interpretation of history clearly expresses the conviction that forgiveness is possible. This is undergirded by God's nature (cf. also Ex. 34:6 f.; Num. 14:8). Knowing that God is willing to forgive makes it easier for man to ask for forgiveness. That the primary motive for forgiveness is found in God's grace and in his willingness to forgive is especially shown in the prayer recorded in Dan. 9:4–19, where the confidence of the intercessor is not based upon the merits of the people but only upon God's faithfulness to his covenant. The same is true of the prayer recorded in Neh. 9:6–37.

Quite another form of the certainty of forgiveness is found in the cultic literature, in which atonement and forgiveness are joined. The repeated phrase "and it will be forgiven him" (Lev. 4:20,26,31,35; 5:10,13,16,18; 6:7; 19:20) is a promise based upon the sacrificial giving of certain gifts to God. Thus forgiveness to a singular degree is placed in the hands of a mediator between God and man. Nevertheless, it is Yahweh, and not the mediator, who determines forgiveness, as the Hebrew original of the phrase "and it shall be forgiven him," makes abundantly clear. The Hebrew does not say, "And he, the priest, will forgive him." The passive construction is often used to designate an act that God performs. Thus the priest performs the act of atonement that is antecedent to forgiveness, but the actual forgiveness itself is not accomplished by the priest. Nevertheless, since correct atonement is essential to the assurance of forgiveness, it is legitimate to speak of a certainty of forgiveness that is mediated through the sacrificial cult.

Psalms

The meaning of forgiveness in The Psalms is especially rich in the variety of its expression. The dating is notoriously difficult, and they are treated together last not because they are latest but because they are all liturgical material. In addition to the abstract terms *salach* and *kphr,* certain figurative expressions are used, such as "He will not remember their sins" (Ps. 25:7) or impute iniquity (Ps. 32:2). In individual cases, even the word for healing is used in connection with sins (Ps. 41:4; 107:20). The literary form of the psalm determines to some extent whether forgiveness is requested (Ps. 25:7,11,18; 51:3 f.,9, 11; 79:8 f.) or whether it is written of in a descriptive way (cf. Micah 7:19) or as something that has already taken place (Ps. 32:5; Isa. 38:17; Ps. 85:2). The psalms, however, also visualize forgiveness as an attribute belonging to the nature of Yahweh (Ps. 65:4; 78:38; 99:8; 103:12; 86:5; and 134). As in the Deuteronomic literature, it is here often based on the history of past experiences (Ps. 78:38; 99:8). Here an interpretation of history derived from experience becomes contemporary and meaningful to the individual.

Forgiveness is seen in The Psalms for the most part as an act of Yahweh that affects a man's life here and now. It is performed either to the individual or to the people or is something he will bring to completion in the future. It clearly has an eschatological meaning in Ps. 85:3 and perhaps also in Ps. 79:9.

In The Psalms, as in the rest of the Old Testament, forgiveness means the removal of the sin that stands between Yahweh and his people or between him and the individual. Since sin is often related to trouble or punishment, forgiveness is often related to the removal of these external troubles. Twice (Ps. 51 and 130), forgiveness becomes virtually a spiritual entity in which the release from sin appears to mean far more than merely the alleviation of sickness and trouble.

One clear indication of the intimate connection that exists between the distressful situation and the freeing from sin is the use of the term "healing" in a number of

places in The Psalms. Thus, Ps. 107:17–20 puts the external healing and the forgiveness of the sins of the sick
side by side. Especially clearly, however, the two are
united in Ps. 103:3 in the words "who pardons all your
sins and heals all afflictions." The prayer for grace and
healing (Ps. 41:4) can be attached quite simply to the
confession of sins. Again the healing is supposed to bring
the external restoration and the removal of sin. Even aside
from the connection between sin and sickness, forgiveness
must have external evidence and reveal itself through
some external event. Thus in Ps. 25:18 and 79:9 the deliverance out of distress and the forgiveness of sins belong
together. Even as God delivered them in the past, this
became an experience of forgiveness for them (Ps. 78:38;
99:8). In the future, God will make manifest his forgiveness through the relaxation of his wrath and the restoration
of the land and its inhabitants (Ps. 85:1 f.).

At times the external restoration recedes sharply behind the freedom from sins granted through forgiveness.
To some extent this is true of Ps. 32:5 but even more so in
Ps. 51 and 130. According to vs. 3 and 4 of Ps. 32, the one
who is praying has been depressed by serious sickness. He
is aware that the reason for this is unconfessed sin:

> When I declared not my sin, my body wasted away
>   through my groaning all day long.
> For day and night thy hand was heavy upon me;
>   my strength was dried up as by the heat of summer.

Through acknowledgment of his sin to God and through a
refusal to hide his iniquity and his confession of the transgression to the Lord, he received forgiveness. The forgiveness and the release from sin were more important for
him than the restoration of his health. However, just be

cause he does not mention it, one should not conclude that the poet received only forgiveness and not restoration of health. As Gunkel puts it: "He [the psalmist], was free from his sufferings and recognized thereby that God had now forgiven him."[14]

Psalm 51, with its deep recognition of sin, in which sin is seen as a power that extended itself upon the individual's life, puts the request for freedom and release from sin in the foreground (cf. vs. 3 f.,9,11). What the poet hopes for, after his forgiveness, is not something external but a pure heart and a new spirit. And yet, even here, the physical aspect is also seen in vs. 8 and 18.[15]

In Ps. 130 the writer cries to God out of mortal illness (cf. vs. 1 f.), yet the forgiveness of his sins is his first request. He begged that the suffering people might receive redemption (v. 7), and this redemption is not in the first place freedom out of distress but out of sin (v. 8).

The psalms see the insight of the sinner into his guilt and the attendant remorse as a prerequisite to forgiveness. The same point of view was also found in the prophets Hosea, Jeremiah, and Deutero-Isaiah. A particularly clear recognition of sin is contained in Ps. 51:3 f.: "For I know my transgressions, and my sin is ever before me. Against thee, thee only, have I sinned, and done that which is evil in thy sight."[16]

In other psalms, too, this deep awareness of sin can be found. The petition for forgiveness follows upon this awareness (vs. 9 f.), and Ps. 86:3,5 are evidence for a constant prayer on the basis of which the psalmist hopes to achieve forgiveness. At times the awareness of sins is only alluded to and not directly expressed (Ps. 130:3).[17]

After the confession of his sins, the confessor may expect to find a hearing with God. In none of the psalms, however, that belong to the confessional type is there evidence of the cultic atonement ritual that is taken for granted in the law. The explanation is probably to be found in the fact that the psalms have separated themselves quite markedly from the cultus. Furthermore, the individual writer's conception of sin is so deep and personalistic (especially Ps. 25 and 51) that the removal of sin from man cannot be viewed in this way. Sin is directed against Yahweh (cf. especially Ps. 41:4) and only against him (Ps. 51:4). Accordingly, it can only be annulled through a word of absolution from Yahweh.[18]

Psalm 65 seems to indicate that at least one writer saw forgiveness as related to the Temple. An interesting condition for forgiveness is given here when the writer says, "When our transgressions prevail over us, thou dost forgive them." The word "prevail" is probably to be understood here as referring to the results of the sin, and not to its nature.[19]

The psalmist grounds his appeal for forgiveness upon his knowledge of God's nature and relationship to man, which he finds abundantly supported in the history of God's people. Since God is by nature gracious and merciful, he will protect his honor by continuing to be gracious. Furthermore, he is also indulgent with human weakness.

The appeal to God's honor is most strongly expressed in the psalms commonly called folk lamentations (Ps. 79:9). The individual lamentation psalms have the same motif (Ps. 25:11). With the appeal to God's honor also lies the promise that in case God answers prayer, the one who is forgiven will declare God's honor.

Yahweh's readiness to forgive is also a result of his recognition that human nature is weak and human life is short. This is the reason given for God's forgiveness of the people in the past (Ps. 78:39). Psalm 130 also contains this motif. General weakness and sinfulness evoke

God's sympathy and incline him toward forgiveness. In comparison to the other motives, this one is farthest away from the center of Israelite thought. It presupposes neither the covenant nor the experience of the people of God. It is, therefore, no accident and should not surprise us that in the Wisdom Literature, whose lack of historical interest is well known, we find this motif used most often. Job appeals to the lot of humanity in a variety of ways in order to get God to be mild toward him (Job 7:17–21; 9:2 f.; 10:20–22; and 14:4–6). Similar thoughts are expressed by Job's friends in order to prove that before God no one is righteous and blameless (chs. 4:17–21; 15:14; and 25:4–6).

It would seem that forgiveness in The Psalms is developed along the same lines that we have noted in the other Old Testament books. For the most part, forgiveness is related to an external confirmation that consists in the alleviation of a distressful situation or sickness. At times, however, this external factor can be seen but dimly in the background. The conception of forgiveness as God's personal act, presupposing man's awareness and confession of sins and remorse, is especially strong in The Psalms. We often find in the writer of The Psalms an intense agony and struggle to achieve forgiveness in his personal experience, but there is never any doubt that God's nature is basically a forgiving one.

This intense personal struggle reflected in the psalms makes them relevant for man's continued search for release from the bondage of sin. The historical material speaks to those whose lives have not yet been wrecked by guilt and thus are open to rational appeals. The psalms speak eloquently to those who have no concept of history anymore. In them, those who feel guilty even for approaching God find their own experience confirmed by the psalmist, who searchingly asks questions, not only of his own soul, and wrestles with his own feelings, but dares to probe the intention and purpose of God. Reading the psalms, mental patients find that there have been others before them whose lives were enveloped by despair. And in the psalms those who have devoted themselves to years of serving God can find out what it means to experience, as David did, the intrusion of sin in all its rudeness and tenacity. Here the reader discovers that he can go beyond the admission, "There is no soundness in my flesh; . . . no health in my bones because of my sin" (Ps. 38:3). He also learns that to hide his sin and not to admit his transgressions results in a wasting away of the body, a drying up of his strength, and the heaviness of the Lord's hand upon him (Ps. 32:3–4). The experience of sin and guilt is not unique to the mental patient or the moralist, much as the reader may think so. Since the beginning of God's redemptive history, there have been those who have experienced the same guilt and condemnation. In their experience of forgiveness we, too, receive hope. The same God who rescued them promises also to rescue us.

THE DYNAMICS OF FORGIVENESS IN THE OLD TESTAMENT

It is a characteristic of our age to analyze the psychological processes that take place in human experience. This tendency has also been carried over into the realm of religious experience. Moreover, we are inclined to apply these same analytic methods of study to the Bible. Such an attempt has disappointing results, because there is such a paucity of evidence, and such an analysis will always reflect more accurately the psychological processes of modern man than those of the Biblical characters involved.

One must raise the question, also, whether we do not have totally different goals and purposes than did the people of the Bible. Ancient man believed in a geocentric universe, and Hebrew man certainly believed in a theocentric universe. To a large extent, modern man is egocentric. One does not need to chastise or excoriate the Greeks to observe the essential correctness of Norman Snaith's statement:

The aim of Hebrew religion was *da' ath Elohim* (the knowledge of God); the aim of Greek thought was *Gnōthi seauton* (know thyself). Between these two there is a great gulf fixed. We do not see that either admits of any compromise. They are fundamentally different in *a priori* assumption, in method of approach, and in final conclusion.[20]

There is no need to exaggerate this difference, but it must be observed with all clarity and frankness. The Greek maxim, after all, was so widespread and so well-known that its absence in Biblical literature is no historical accident. Snaith, indeed, insists that there is the widest possible difference between these two approaches. "They are poles apart in attitude and method. The Hebrew system starts with God. The only true wisdom is knowledge of God." Thus, man can never know himself, what he is and what his relationship is to the world, unless he first learns to know God and learns submission to God's will. The Greek, on the other hand, starts with the knowledge of man and seeks to rise to an understanding of the ways and nature of God through what is called man's higher nature. According to the Bible, man has no higher nature except he be born of the spirit.[21]

Our study would seem to support this thesis. We have repeatedly noted that forgiveness is born of God and manifested again and again through the saving acts of God in history. It is supported also by the fact that God is almost universally and exclusively portrayed as the forgiving agent. Man cannot forgive himself unless God first forgives him. He cannot know himself until he is known of God.

This, however, dare not preclude some interest on our part in the psychological dimensions of experiencing forgiveness and the obligation to pursue, as far as possible, the human side of this experience. This is particularly urgent when we view forgiveness not as a formal act but as God's personal act by which he seeks to restore fellowship between God and man. Viewed in this way, it involves a definite personal participation of man in this act of God. Walther Eichrodt has said: "Here man must be deeply involved, in order that a real renewal of fellowship take place."[22]

Throughout the history of Israel, it was clearly understood that man could not merely hope for forgiveness and pray for it but also that he must humble himself before God, confess his wrongs, and have a sincere desire to change his ways. In the liturgy of the day of fasting, as also in the presentation of sacrifices, it is assumed that remorse and confession of sins are natural aspects of the request for forgiveness (Josh. 7:10–21; Lev. 5:5; 16:21; Num. 5:7; cf. I Sam. 7:5 ff.; Job 42:8). Both the individual and the collective penitential psalms, whose origin lies far back in the history of the people, confirm this observation (Ps. 25:7; 32:5; 38:19; 41:5; 51:6 ff.; 65:4; 130:3 ff.; Lam. 3:40 ff.).

A variety of expressions describe man's responsibility in this process: to seek Yahweh (II Sam. 12:16; 21:1; Hos. 5:6,15; Zeph. 2:3), to inquire after him (Amos 5:4,6; Hos. 10:12; Isa. 55:6), to humble one's self before him

(I Kings 21:29; II Kings 22:19; Lev. 26:31; II Chron. 7:14; 12:6 ff.; etc.), to incline one's heart toward Yahweh (I Sam. 7:3), to become mellow of heart (II Kings 22:19), and to confess one's self to Yahweh (I Kings 8:33,35). External expressions of this inner feeling are weeping and wailing, fasting, rending of clothes, sleeping on the ground, being covered with ashes, etc. The prophets were concerned that these external acts never degenerate into mere rituals, and used countless expressions to indicate a genuine return to God. Ezekiel pleads, "Get yourselves a new heart and a new spirit" (ch. 18:31), while both Jeremiah (ch. 4:4) and Deuteronomy (ch. 10:16) speak of the circumcision of the heart. Both Jeremiah (ch 4:3) and Hosea (ch. 10:12) speak of cutting a new furrow in fallow ground. Alongside this, there are also images out of the cultic speech: "to wash one's heart of all evil" (Jer. 4:14), "to be purified and cleansed" (Isa. 1:16; cf. Ezek. 36:25).

Eichrodt observes that

the multitude of these expressions shows how seriously the call to personal decision in connection with forgiveness was taken in Israel and thus supports from another side God's personal involvement in the act of forgiveness.[23]

All of this can be subsumed under the word *shub,* meaning "to return." The Hebrew word, which thus describes man's responsibility, or at least man's attitude toward this, carries the connotation of turning toward something. Usually it is assumed that the man will turn away from sin or idolatry and toward God. This describes the attitude and action, regardless of how elementary it may be, that shows the nature of man's response to God. God does not force himself upon man—he takes the initiative even in repentance—but if man does not respond to his wooing, then forgiveness is impossible.

The Hebrew religion did not leave in doubt the question whether men actually had experienced forgiveness. One cannot be accused of "psychologizing" the Bible when one observes that the psychological dimensions of forgiveness are given full play alongside the theological dimension. Although the Bible does not begin with the human side of the divine-human encounter, it does not neglect the human aspects. God's actions take place on the plane of history and directly affect human experience. This aspect of forgiveness, however, brings us directly to the cultic dimensions of Israel's life.

The Cultus and Forgiveness

The cultus was, to a large extent, a reenactment of the history of Israel, and it sought to make the redemption of Israel from Egypt meaningful to their own experience. On the matter of guilt and sin, the ritual was so dramatic that it must have been extremely powerful from a psychological point of view. The ideas of ransom and substitution figure largely as the means by which forgiveness becomes a reality in the life of the individual Israelite. For the idea of substitution is common to the forms of redemption that occur in the Old Testament; man gives something in order to receive another thing in its place: where sin is concerned, man exchanges his sins for a new life.[24]

In the sacrificial ritual, substitution is most concretely expressed. It is at the basis of the burnt offering (Lev. 1:4) as well as the sin offering (ch. 4:20) and the guilt offering (ch. 5:16). Jacob offers some interesting examples of the widespread influence of the idea of substitution in the Semitic world, citing an Accadian text, which reads:

The lamb is the substitute for man; for his life, he shall deliver the lamb:
The lamb's head shall he deliver for the man's head.

The neck of the lamb shall he deliver for the
    neck of the man,
The breast of the lamb for the breast of the man
    shall he deliver.[25]

The sealing of a treaty between two eighth-century princes
included the following words at the time of the victim's
immolation:

The head is not a ram's head, it is Mati' ilu's head, the head
of his sons, of his great ones, of the people of this country.
If the aforesaid sin against these provisions, just as this ram's
head is removed, may the thigh of the aforesaid, of his children, of his great ones, of the people of his land be removed.[26]

It would seem apparent that there is here a symbolic
transmission of particular life to the victim in order to
keep the totality of life safe. Perhaps no other passage
captures this as forcefully as Deut. 21:1–9. If a man is
found murdered and it is not known who slew him, the
elders of the city nearest to the spot where he is found
are to take a heifer down to a valley and there break the
neck of the heifer. The elders shall wash their hands over
the heifer testifying,

Our hands did not shed this blood, neither did our eyes see it
shed. Forgive, O Lord, thy people Israel, whom thou hast redeemed, and set not the guilt of innocent blood in the midst of
thy people Israel; but let the guilt of blood be forgiven them.
(Deut. 21:7 f.)

In order to prevent the kind of incident occasioned by
Achan, this ritual allowed the heifer to die for the sin committed by an unknown person.

    That forgiveness is also practiced among the people
themselves is clear from the moving story of Joseph. How

easy it would have been for him to retaliate against his brothers for their misdeeds! And how they feared that he would! Yet Joseph was a true Israelite and forgave the sin of his brothers. They asked for forgiveness, and Joseph recognized that to withhold it from them would be to assume that he was in the place of God (Gen. 50:19). Far from asserting that only God can forgive, he says that only He can withhold forgiveness from man. Joseph recognized that although they meant evil against him, God had a good purpose in it, and he would not now frustrate that divine purpose by withholding forgiveness from them. Thus the Old Testament not only presents us with a profound doctrine of forgiveness but also offers concrete illustrations from human life on how forgiveness was experienced within the life of the covenant community.[27]

Part Two

FORGIVENESS
IN PRE-CHRISTIAN JUDAISM

Chapter IV

Sin and the Day of Atonement

A study of any aspect of pre-Christian Judaism must recognize that certain recent discoveries have changed many traditional interpretations. A designation such as "normative" Judaism must be used with caution, since there is debate on where and when such a phenomenon arose. The chronological limits of this period are vague. At one end it is almost certain that The Book of Daniel belongs in this period. It is therefore artificial to use the term "intertestamental" to designate a period of time lying between the Old and the New Testaments. On the other end it is well known that the Rabbinic material, although not written down in final form until several centuries after the beginning of the Christian era, contains material dating from the pre-Christian era. Nevertheless, the weight of tradition and the precedents set by scholarship are so ponderous that for the purpose of this study we may be permitted to follow the precedents even after our acknowledgment of the problems concurrent with such usage.

We shall attempt to trace certain constant factors already observed in the Old Testament and some deviations from the Old Testament conceptions of sin and forgiveness. The first question that concerns us is: To what extent is guilt or consciousness of sin an important aspect of the piety of this period? We shall then turn to a consideration of the ways in which forgiveness is attained. The agents of forgiveness, the motives of forgiveness, and, finally, the limits of forgiveness will in turn be considered.[1]

THE CONSCIOUSNESS OF SIN

It has been observed by A. Büchler that Judaism followed the Old Testament by taking sin seriously. Sin was a fact of life for the rabbis, and they assumed an identification between keeping God's laws and hearing his voice.[2] Solomon Schechter in his treatment of Rabbinic theology states that their idea of sin is in harmony with their conception of man's duty toward the law, and that any deviation from the ways of God was considered defiance and rebellion or sin.[3] George F. Moore in his classic study of Judaism says:

Sin is in fact a religious, not primarily a moral, conception. It is an offense against God, and the gravest are offenses against his holiness, that is, his godhead itself. . . .

In Judaism, where the two-fold law by which all spheres and relations of life were regulated was the revealed will of God, the doing of anything expressly or by implication forbidden in the law, or the neglect of anything commanded in it, was necessarily regarded as an offense against the divine lawgiver.[4]

With such a profound and inclusive conception of sin, it is understandable that the consciousness of sin could pervade the totality of Judaism.

A further historical development that certainly contributed to this awareness of sins was the demise of the Jewish nation-state as seen most painfully in the exile. In view of the prophetic warnings and call to repentance that preceded the exile, it was inevitable that the sensitive spirits within Judaism would see the exile as a punishment from God for their individual and corporate sins.[5] A most moving testimony to such sentiments is found in the prayer recorded in Dan., ch. 9. It is typical of Jewish religion that such a prayer can be ascribed to a just and upright man. It portrays forcefully the distinction that exists between the righteousness of God and the sinfulness of man. The refrain

We have sinned and done wrong and rebelled and turned aside. . . . We have not listened to thy servants the prophets (Dan. 9:5 f.)

stands in the best tradition of confessional and penitential literature. Alongside of it stands the greatness of God, his righteousness and his mercy.

To thee, O Lord, belongs righteousness, but to us confusion of face,
To us, O Lord, belongs confusion of fact, to our kings, to our princes, and to our fathers, because we have sinned against thee.
To the Lord our God belong mercy and forgiveness; because we have rebelled against him, and have not obeyed the voice of the Lord our God. (Vs. 7–10.)

Four times we find the words "we have sinned" (vs. 5,8,11, 15). The writer specifically indicates that he was confessing not only the general sins of Israel but "confessing my sin and the sin of my people Israel" (v. 20). The recognition and confession of personal and corporate sin, the awareness that forgiveness comes from God and that unless such forgiveness comes, God's people will continue to be a byword among all the surrounding peoples (v. 16), but above all the cry of an anguished heart:

O Lord, hear; O Lord, forgive; O Lord, give heed and act; delay not, for thy own sake, O my God, because thy city and thy people are called by thy name (v. 19)

lead us to designate this prayer as one of the finest penitential prayers to be found in any religion.

The penitential prayer must be seen as a type that is at home in Jewish piety. It is not extraneous. Its presence in the Old Testament opens the door to its expansion in postexilic Judaism. In The Book of Ezra (ch. 9), it is focused on one particular sin, that of intermarriage, but in other parts of the Old Testament it is more broadly conceived (I Kings, ch. 8). The sense of sin expressed in these prayers is both corporate and private; it springs out of personal actions and also represents a response to historical events viewed as divine punishment.

A special place belongs to The Prayer of Manasseh. It gives expression to the sense of sin in the nation:

I am unworthy to look up and see the height
    of heaven
 because of the multitude of my iniquities.
I am weighted down with many an iron fetter,
    so that I am rejected because of my sins,
    and I have no relief.

(Vs. 9–10.)

Although there is no evidence that this prayer ever existed in Hebrew, scholars are agreed that it comes from a pre-Christian period. The earliest evidence of its existence is the Syriac Didascalia, dating from the third century A.D.

and the fourth-century Apostolic Constitutions. Its popularity in Protestantism can be attributed to Luther's high regard for it.[6]

The outline of the penitential prayer seems to have become formalized. It begins with an ascription to God and praise for the wonderful works he has done to the patriarchs or past generations of Israelites. In The Prayer of Manasseh we are explicitly told that repentance is not appointed for the righteous,

for Abraham and Isaac and Jacob, who did not sin against thee, but thou hast appointed repentance for me, who am a sinner. (V. 8.)

After a description of his sins comes the petition for forgiveness:

> I have sinned, O Lord, I have sinned,
> and I know my transgressions.
> I earnestly beseech thee,
> forgive me, O Lord, forgive me!
>
> (Vs. 12–13.)

God is a God of those who repent, and it is his nature to forgive. Yet such a consciousness of sins is also closely related to the petitioner's sense of personal worth, expressed in this prayer by the words:

In me thou wilt manifest thy goodness;
> for, unworthy as I am, thou wilt save me in thy great mercy. (V. 14.)

A similar sentiment is expressed in The Prayer of Azariah:

We are brought low this day in all the world because of our sins.

And at this time there is no prince, or prophet, or leader,
no burnt offering, or sacrifice, or oblation, or incense,
no place to make an offering before thee or to find mercy.
Yet with a contrite heart and a humble spirit may we be
accepted.

(Vs. 14–16.)

A similar pattern is found in the book of Baruch, where
the prayer of confession is prescribed to be read when
they make their "confession in the house of the Lord on
the days of the feasts and at appointed seasons" (ch. 1:14).

It would seem from this that we are justified in saying that "a deep and for the most part commendable consciousness of sin pervades this period."[7] To be sure, the
penitential psalms do not express the whole of Jewish
piety, but they do represent an important and significant
element and perhaps also a popular element. The relationship between popular piety and these expressions is,
however, complex. Most of the penitential psalms include
references to both the sins of the people and the individual. Mathematically, the sins of the individuals constitute
national sin. It is all the more striking that the Hasidim,
the more scrupulous Jews, were apparently not much
troubled by an oppressive burden of guilt. There is much
more evidence for a naïve joy about their own righteousness and confidence that God's continuing love will not
fail (Ps. 103). Perhaps a general consciousness of sin did
not exist among these people to any great extent.[8] Yet
writers of sensitive spirit or conscience did give literary
outlet to their own convictions, and no doubt they sought
thereby to influence the thinking of the people in the
same direction.

Consciousness of guilt does find expression in the popular prayers. For example, the Shemoneh Esreh, although

somewhat more recent than the Shema and considered *the* prayer by the Jews, contains this petition:

> Forgive us, O our Father, for we have sinned; pardon us,
> O our King, for we have transgressed; for thou dost
> pardon and forgive. Blessed art thou, O Lord,
> who art gracious, and dost abundantly forgive.[9]

Every Israelite, even women, slaves, and children had to repeat this prayer three times a day. According to a reliable account, it was instituted by an authoritative synagogue toward the end of the first century A.D. This points toward usage earlier than the first century, although to what extent is not known. K. G. Kuhn, an authority on Jewish writings proposes that it could be dated as early as 100 B.C.[10] What is of importance for our study is that everyone thrice daily prayed for the forgiveness of sins. Thus the consciousness of sin was more or less reawakened three times during a day, but alongside of such awakening of guilt there is also the firm conviction that God's nature is forgiving and that he answers the prayer of those who are repentant. The fifth petition deals with repentance, thus preparing the way for the sixth petition, which deals with forgiveness.

THE DAY OF ATONEMENT

Without question the Day of Atonement was the high point of the Jewish year. It is called "the feast, fast day" thus expressing the two aspects of the Yom Kippur: the splendor of the festival, the joyous anticipation and acceptance of forgiveness, together with the severity of the fast, the prohibition of all labor and a prescribed fivefold self-affliction. Only on this day of the year did the high priest enter the Holy of Holies. Then he laid aside the resplendent eight golden garments that he wore for the rest of the year and donned instead four simple linen garments that he used for the most important part of his service that day.

The climax of the service came when the high priest burned incense in the Holy of Holies. The Sadducees differed from the traditional order in some of the details, and since some of the high priests were suspected of sympathizing with the Sadducees, the high priest had to take a solemn oath promising to officiate in strict accordance with Jewish law.

The events of the day may be briefly summarized. At daybreak the high priest killed the lamb for the perpetual morning sacrifice, the blood of which was sprinkled on the outer altar. Then came the daily offering of incense in the temple. Moving again to the outer altar, the high priest offered the prescribed parts of the lamb along with his own cake offering. Then followed the additional sacrifice prescribed in Num., ch. 29, for the festivals, except that the high priest's bullock and the male goat were omitted.

Now the Atonement Day ritual proper began. The high priest changed into his white linen garments, approached the young bullock, which was his own sin offering, and placed his hands on the bullock's head and made confession of sin for himself. As he pronounced the ineffable name, the priests and the people in the court prostrated themselves and called out: "Blessed be his glorious Kingdom for ever and ever."

to p. 42

Leviticus 16:7 specifies that two goats shall be standing ready "at the door of the tent of meeting," which meant that in the temple they stood north of the altar. Lots were cast, and by this means one went to the Lord, the other to Azazel. Azazel designated the rock in the wilderness from which the scapegoat was hurled to its death but also came to be used as a surrogate for all that is sinful and evil. After the casting of the lot, the high priest placed his hands on the bullock's head and made confession for the whole house of Aaron (the priests). A second time when they heard him pronounce the name of God, they fell down and worshiped. He then slew the bullock and received its blood in a vessel, which he placed outside.

Leo Jung describes the next step as follows:

Paraphrase

Now came the most solemn part of the service; the high priest entered the Holy of Holies for the purpose of offering up the incense before the golden ark which contained the Tables of the Covenant, and the populace outside waited with bated breath for his safe return and especially during the period of the second Temple when they had reason to be afraid that a faithless high priest might render their service improperly, and might himself be punished for such treachery, and might fail to bring the eagerly awaited forgiveness for the people of Israel. So great was the joy of the people after the safe return of the high priest from the Holy of Holies, that the afternoon of the Day of Atonement in Palestine became an occasion of popular rejoicing, as described in Ta'anith 26b.[11]

The high priest now took the vessel containing the blood, returned it to the Holy of Holies, and sprinkled it eight times toward the Ark of the Covenant. Once he sprinkled blood on the mercy seat, and seven times he cast it on the front of the Ark to "cover" the sins of the priests. He returned to the court, and having set the blood of the bull on a stand, he went out to perform the ritual of atonement for the people.

The next step was the selection of the goats by lot. A special urn for the two lots was provided, and as the priest placed his hand in the urn he drew out the lots, one inscribed "For the Lord" and the other, "For Azazel." As he brought down the lots in his hand on the heads of the rams he cried to one, "To the Lord" and tied a red ribbon onto the other goat for Azazel.

The priest then slaughtered the other goat, and carrying its blood, he entered the sanctuary for the third time to sprinkle the Ark in behalf of the people. Returning to the nave, he exchanged the vessel of goat's blood for the one with the blood of the bull and sprinkled the veil seven times, facing the Ark. Then, once again taking the goat's blood, he did the same. After that, he poured the remainder of the blood together into the two vessels and proceeded to anoint the horns of the golden altar of incense which stood before the veil and symbolized the prayers of Israel (Ex. 30:1–10). Using his fingers, he sprinkled it with blood in order to remove all of Israel's uncleanness from it.

Special significance must be attached to the custom of the scapegoat. The widespread use of such symbolic means in other cultures and the antiquity of such practices makes it hard to deny the antiquity of the Hebrew practice. Indeed, some see in it the oldest part of the whole proceedings of the Day of Atonement. The fact that both goats are to be purchased the same day and to have similar if not identical characteristics indicates that their task is a common one. The one goat gives its life to atone for the people, while the other becomes the symbolic bearer of the sins of the people into the wilderness, the place of all evil. As the ritual developed, to assure the people that the goat would never again return, he was killed in the wilderness by throwing him from a high cliff. The high priest confessed the sins of the people, laying his hands on the goat. He then turned the goat over to the man who would lead it away. The people, however, increasingly began to participate in the departure of the goat, pulling out its hair, spitting on it, pricking it, and shouting, "Begone, Begone" (Yoma 6:4; cf. Barnabas 7:8).

From a psychological viewpoint, such an experience must have been profoundly moving. The drama and tension of the ritual itself would almost assure this. Of most interest to us is the way in which the sin and guilt are objectively removed from one's presence. The corporate aspects of it are also of great importance. The people say to the goat, "Begone," but in effect they are saying to all their sins: "Begone." With the removal of the goat, they are able to assure themselves that the guilt has been removed. Those who have doubts and continue to wallow in their guilt could be asked: "Did you not see the goat leave, carrying your sin?" Whatever may be the exact background and meaning of the constituent parts of this day, whatever may be the historical and form-critical background of the material that reports it to us, there is unanimous agreement that the Day of Atonement represents a unique festival. Philo described it as the greatest of the feasts (*On the Special Laws* II, xxxii). He no doubt spoke the conviction of many pious Jews. For with the declaration of forgiveness and the restoration of fellowship with God and with one's fellowman, one could look forward with joy to the coming of the New Year. Sadness and joy are mingled together on the Day of Atonement, because there is a sorrow that leads to repentance and that brings inexpressible joy. It was said: "There were no happier days for Israel than the 15th of Ab and the Day of Atonement."

CHAPTER V

The Place of Forgiveness
of Sins at Qumran

Within Judaism we must pay special attention to the sect
at Qumran because it had great interest in guilt and forgiveness, but had suspended its participation in the traditional ways of removing guilt. The writings of this community which have been discovered, widely studied, and
abundantly described contain a remarkable amount of material on both sin and forgiveness. Especially in the psalms
or hymns of Qumran we have some of the most moving
literature of Judaism.

First, we must consider the background against which
these assertions on sin and forgiveness are made. A re-
current theme in the Qumran literature, especially in the
hymns, is the frailty of man.[1] The writer of one such hymn
asks: "But I, a creature of clay, what am I? I, kneaded
with water, and for what am I esteemed?" (iii:23–24). In
a somewhat more impersonal vein, the question is asked:

And, indeed, what is he, man? He is earth! From clay was he
nipped off and to dust is his return. . . . And I am but dust
and ashes. (x:3–5.)

Man's origin is in the dust, and

> the knowledge of human weakness is developed into a conviction that man is entirely base, and finally into an almost pathological abhorrence of human nature.[2]

> And as for me [I am] a creature of clay and kneaded with water; the foundation of shamefulness, and the source of impurity; the crucible of iniquity, and the edifice of sin; the erring spirit and am perverted, devoid of understanding. (i:21–23.)

Similar imagery occurs in another hymn with slightly different combinations:

> Seeing [man] is a structure of dust and kneaded in water, whose foundation is a crucible of iniquity, a nakedness of shamefulness, a source of impurity. And a perverted spirit hath dominion over him. (xiii:14–16.)

It is clear that these writers derive their view of man from the creation narrative, and they stress the "raw material" used in creating man. The deepest evidence for man's perversity, however, comes from his sin. Here ethical dualism is of greater significance even than metaphysical components.

> Who is he [that is] flesh [who can work] like this, and who is he a creature of clay to exalt [Thy] wonders? For he is steeped in sin from the womb and unto old age, [he is] amid treacherous guilt. For, verily I know that righteousness belongs not to a mortal, nor is integrity of way to a son of man. (iv:29–30.)

While the theme is most forcefully expressed in the hymns, the same note is also struck in the Manual of Discipline:

> I belong to sinful mankind, to the community of sinful mortals. My misdeeds, my trespasses, my sins and the badness of my

heart belong by right to the fellowship of worms and to those who roam in the darkness. (1QS XI:9–10.)

Not only is the view of unregenerate man "more pessimistic than one usually encounters in Hebrew-Jewish writings,"[3] but the human problem is seen primarily as one of guilt.

But I, trembling and shivering have seized me and all my bones are broken and my heart hath melted as wax before the fire. And my knees drip as waters that are poured down a slope, for I have remembered my guilts together with the treachery of my fathers, when wicked men rose against thy covenant and tyrants [rose] against thy word. (iv:33–35.)

Those who do not join the sect or avail themselves of God's grace are called "sons of guilt" (v:7; vi:18–19,30; vii:11). The fountain of understanding and the counsel of truth is withheld from them "because of their guilt" (v:25–26). In their guilt his enemies rob the writer of strength and cause his spirit to stumble (v:36). The writer refers to his own "anguish of guilt" (xi:20) and describes his enemies as "wallowing in guilt" (vi:22) and himself as "wallowing in the pollution" (of guilt) (xvii:19).[4]

Although this concentration on the perversity of man is not found in the Old Testament, and man is rarely described as a "worm," nor is his origin in the dust used to denigrate him, these hymns do share one thing at least with the Old Testament psalms. They are written after the deliverance, and it is from this vantage point that they are to be interpreted. Redemption through the Lord's grace opens up the full magnitude of man's rebellion. Guilt is the screen on which forgiveness is displayed.

But whenever I remember the might of thy hand with the overflowing of Thy compassion, I am fortified; yea I rise, and my spirit hath held firmly [its] position in the face of a blow, for I lean on thy loving kindness and the overflowing of Thy compassion. For Thou atonest a sin, and cleansest man from guilt through righteousness, not for the sake of man [but for Thy glory]. (iv:35 f.)

This theme of deliverance and thanksgiving for the deliverance is found repeatedly. God did not judge him according to his guilt (v:5), and the writer is especially grateful for God's forgiveness (v:1 ff.). He is convinced that God will raise up a remnant among His people and a survivor in His inheritance, people whom God will purify so as to be cleansed from guilt,

for all their deeds are in Thy truth and with Thy loving kindness Thou judgest them; with the overflowing of Thy compassion, and the abundance of forgiveness. (vi:8–9.)

He has refused to take refuge in the strength of men, in his own wisdom, nor has he trusted in his flesh; rather, he has placed his whole faith in God's forgiveness (vii:17–18). Forgiveness is a mark of the true children of God (vii:30), and thus God's forgiveness becomes an object of the writer's thanksgiving (vii:35).

In a great hymn of deliverance the writer describes how he found that God did not reject him but through loving-kindness led him to help when the throes of death encompassed him and infernal pains were upon his bed.

Thou hast not forsaken my hope and in the presence of calamity Thou hast upheld my spirit. For Thou hast firmly established my spirit and Thou knowest my intent, And in my distress Thou hast comforted me and I delight in Thy pardon and I shall be comforted over the first transgression. (ix:11–13.)

Later in the same psalm (the text is not fully extant) the writer seems to be saying that God gave him a "just rebuke," but that when God does so, his footsteps bring "abundant forgiveness" and there is an overflowing of compassion when God judges him (ix:33–34). Discipline and fatherhood are here related, which is the more striking since it appears to be the only place where God is addressed as father in these texts.[5] In God's goodness there is "abundance of forgiveness" (xi:9), and pardoning sin is seen as one of God's activities (xvi:16).

Our survey would seem to indicate that for the writer sinfulness and frailty form an entity; creatureliness and guilt are one and the same thing. Yet this conclusion is arrived at only after salvation, or deliverance, has been attained. Forgiveness is not forced out of the picture through any obsession with man's creaturely sinfulness. Some attention is devoted to the sins committed prior to repentance and conversion, but much stress is still laid on the present guilt and sinfulness. Another factor that seems to be missing is the duality of one's own desires and accomplishments. There appears no tension between willing and doing. In fact, sin is seen primarily as obeying the law and it is likely that transgression of the law was the primary focus of the confessions on the annual day of covenant renewal practiced by the covenanters.[6]

Totally missing in these psalms is any attempt to excuse one's behavior or to compare it with that of others. In II Esdras, ch. 3, the writer admits that they have sinned, but surely, he goes on, not any more than some others; why, then, should they get such serious punishment? No appeal is made to his relative innocence in these psalms. There can be no doubt that the writers go beyond the Biblical material in the vividness with which they portray both man's sinfulness and his creatureliness. The only instances in the Old Testament where man is described as a "worm" clearly indicate that such a low view of man is decisively rejected (Job 25:6; Ps. 22:6; Isa. 41:14). Yet the opposite extreme, which maintains that man can save himself, is also rejected. Finally, it is clear that the Qumran sect had found a solution to the problem of guilt and sin. J. Licht has observed that for the Qumran writer

divine forgiveness is practically identical with the wonderful and exceptional mercy that God grants to His elect; and the phrase "many forgivings" (ix:13; x:21; xi:31) is used in DST [Thanksgiving Scroll] as a synonym for "multitude of mercy." The distinction between the concept of forgiveness and the more general concept of grace is obliterated.[7]

It would be wrong to accuse the people at Qumran of overstressing guilt, because there is evidence that the dynamics of forgiveness were fully operative.

Although they spoke highly of the Day of Atonement, which must have had special significance for them, they had observed a special day of covenant renewal in which penitence held a special place. The Day of Atonement is called a "festival of rest. . . the day of fasting, their Sabbath of rest" (1QpHab xi:6 ff.), and apparently it was on such a high festival that the conflict between the teacher of the community and the decadent priests came into the open. Yet they apparently continued to observe the Day of Atonement (CD vi:19).

Of central importance, however, was the special festival of the covenant, which is described in 1QS I,18–II,18. The liturgy of this service included a declaration of the sins of Israel (I, 22–24a) and then a confession of sin spoken by the congregation (I, 24b–II,1):

We have acted perversely, we have transgressed, we have sinned, we have done wickedly, ourselves and our fathers before us, in that we have gone counter to the truth. God has been right to bring His judgment upon us and upon our fathers.

Howbeit, always from ancient times He has also bestowed His mercies upon us, and so will He do for all time to come. (Gaster's translation.)

According to Manfred Weise, who has studied this matter in detail, the confession is to be spoken by all members of the community, not only the novitiates. Furthermore, it does not contain anything distinctive to Qumran but could have been taken from Judaism as known to us from other sources. He concludes that neither form nor content leads us to conclude that the group created it, but that "it represents generally Jewish liturgical material." Behind it lies a cultic practice represented also in such materials as Neh. 9:32 f.; Ezra 9:6 f.; and Dan. 9:4–19.[8]

We see, then, that apart from the Temple and the priesthood, they had been able to form a society in which mutual forgiveness was practiced and in which the forgiveness of God himself formed the foundation for their corporate life. It is in this area rather than any purely formal aspects that the deepest ties seem to exist between the first Christian community and the Qumran sectarians. The link that would appear to relate them most directly is John the Baptist.

To the question of whether the consciousness of sin is alive in pre-Christian Judaism we would need to answer in the affirmative.[9] We have seen evidence of this in the prayers of Judaism, in the form of literature known as penitential psalms, and we have seen it in the literature of Qumran. Above all, it appears also in the cultic celebration of the Day of Atonement, the existence of which cannot be explained apart from its intent to deal with the consciousness of sin.

CHAPTER VI

The Agent and Motive of Forgiveness

THE AGENT OF FORGIVENESS

As in the Old Testament, so in Judaism major emphasis falls on the assertion or conviction that God forgives. Mead has observed: "The unassailable bastion of a real belief in forgiveness was God, who loves the people he has created and therefore shows them mercy."[1] The various strands of literature in Judaism support this contention. For example, in the "wisdom literature" type, Sirach, ch. 18, gives expression to the conviction that God forgives his people.

> Who can measure his majestic power?
>> And who can fully recount his mercies?
> The Lord is patient with them [men]
>> and pours out his mercy upon them.
> He sees and recognizes that their end will be evil;
>> therefore he grants them forgiveness in abundance.
> Before judgment, examine yourself,
>> and in the hour of visitation you will find forgiveness.
>
>> (Vs. 5, 11–12, 20.)

Similarly, the penitential prayer of Manasseh, after describing the awesome majesty of God, continues:

Yet immeasurable and unsearchable is thy promised mercy,
    for thou art the Lord Most High,
of great compassion, long-suffering, and very merciful,
    and repentest over the evils of men.

(Vs. 6–7.)

The tract describing the ritual for the Day of Atonement concludes on a note of gratitude:

R. Akiba said: Blessed are ye, O Israel. Before whom are ye made clean and who makes you clean? Your Father in Heaven; as it is written, And I will sprinkle clean water upon you and ye shall be clean. And again it says, O Lord the hope of Israel; as the Mikweh [Hope] cleanses the unclean, so does the Holy One, blessed be he, cleanse Israel. (Yoma, Danby text, 8:9.)

Where does this emphasis on God's forgiveness and mercy come from? Wilhelm Bousset believed that it is a psychological compensation motivated by the feeling that one cannot be certain of God's mercy and forgiveness. At no other place in Jewish religion, he maintains, do we see such a lengthy discussion of the mercy, grace, and goodness of God.

Behind all of the confessions of a good and merciful God lies the trembling fear of an inconceivably high and harsh God who is judge over death and life, to whom no man can render satisfaction, who is the giver of the law with its demands and which will not allow the conscience to rest. Precisely the number of attempts to ground the mercy of God in his nature shows its inner insecurity.[2]

The position of Bousset has been submitted to penetrating criticism by, among others, Erik Sjöberg. Perhaps most important, it should be noted that Bousset restricted

his analysis too much to the apocalyptic and pseudepi-
graphic literature, although even in that literature his
observations do not wholly apply. Rather, it seems that
Judaism built upon earlier Old Testament insights that God
is by nature forgiving. Tension exists, to be sure, between
his forgiving and his justice, but this tension is to a large
extent overcome through man's repentance.

If Judaism agrees with the Old Testament in affirming
God's forgiveness, it appears to stress more the position
that forgiveness is God's prerogative. Many students of
Judaism have concluded that God alone forgives. G. F.
Moore begins his chapter entitled "Motives of Forgiveness"
with the sentence: "Forgiveness is a prerogative of God
which he shares with no other and deputes to none."[3]
Israel Abrahams recognized no difference between the
Old and New Testaments on the matter of forgiveness,
except it be that Jesus claimed the function of mediator-
ship between God and man in the matter of forgiveness.

The prophet . . . might bring men to forgiveness; he did not
bring forgiveness to men; it was not his to bring. . . . On the
whole it is true to assert that [in Rabbinic theology] the principle was left intact that God and God alone is the object of
worship and the sole and immediate source of forgiveness.[4]

Solomon Schechter, another authority on Rabbinic theology, also says: "The prerogative of granting pardon is
entirely in the hands of God, every mediator being excluded from this prerogative,"[5] while Paul Billerbeck, in
his commentary on the New Testament, says: "The forgiving of sins remains in all of our literature exclusively
the right of God."[6] In spite of the unanimity of these
impressive authorities, it should be noted that their argu-
ments are based primarily on silence. The sources stress

that God forgives, but as Mead has correctly observed: "It is hard to find statements pertinent to the issue whether *only* God may forgive."[7] What must be recalled here is that both Christian and Jewish sources expect the faithful to forgive their fellowmen. How can such forgiveness be expected if to God alone belongs the prerogative to forgive? Nevertheless, the fact that no tradition exists ascribing to the Messiah the authority and power to forgive sins seems to support the assumption that in Judaism the power to forgive sins was attributed alone to God.[8]

THE MOTIVES FOR FORGIVENESS

Why does God forgive? In the Old Testament we saw certain indications that human weakness played a part in God's reason for forgiveness. Yet this does not seem to be the dominant motive. Erik Sjöberg finds that there are three dominant motives for forgiveness: (1) God forgives for the sake of the patriarchs; (2) God forgives because it is consistent with his nature, honor, and being; and (3) God forgives because he is loving and merciful.[9] Of these three motives the last two are the most prominent.

The appeal to the patriarchs is in effect an appeal to history. God's faithfulness has been shown in establishing and keeping the covenant. In any event, it is clear that "men may seek of God the forgiveness of sins 'for the sake of the fathers'; but they cannot claim to have their demerit offset by the merit of the fathers."[10]

It has been customary to minimize the importance that ignorance has as a motive for forgiveness. Yet there are Biblical texts that clearly support the position that man's ignorance is a factor in God's forgiveness. David Daube in an incisive study has called our attention to the fact that the first of the Eighteen Benedictions is not a prayer for forgiveness or for the power to repent, but a prayer for knowledge, discernment, and understanding.[11] In Jewish law there is a definite development stipulating mercy toward the ignorant and stressing severity of punishment and difficulty of atonement for the willful transgression. In Acts 22:30 to 23:1 ff., Paul is not considered guilty of reviling the high priest Ananias because he pleads innocence on the basis of his ignorance of the fact that Ananias was the high priest. By the first century Eliezer the Great even interpreted Num. 15:25–26 as teaching that even the deliberate presumptuous sins of the community are treated by God as sins committed in error. According to Daube this section is the means

by which nowadays the entire service of the Day of Atonement is placed under the *motif* of forgiveness on the ground of deeper ignorance. The very first quotation from Scripture in this service is the following: "And it shall be forgiven all the congregation of Israel and the stranger that sojourneth among them, seeing that all people are in ignorance."[12]

Daube concludes that this development may well have its roots in independent Jewish tradition rather than in Greek-Hellenistic influence.[13] God's forgiving nature, his faithfulness to his promises to the patriarchs, and his awareness that men are ignorant constitute the motives for his forgiveness in this period.

THE PROCESS OF FORGIVENESS

In Judaism an elaborate cultus had developed in which atonement and forgiveness played a dominant role. The emphasis apparently was on atonement, yet the two were not sharply differentiated. Such a formal structure was, of course, open to abuse. Already, in the Old Testament, prophets and priests criticized those who placed their trust in sacrifices alone without an attendant attitude of repentance and a change of behavior. During the inter-testamental period this was indeed a live issue.

The Old Testament rules out forgiveness for a sin "committed with a high hand" (Num. 15:30). The context seems to indicate that ritual atonement is not efficacious in such cases. In Tannaitic sources, likewise, we have such statements as:

> If in these things he transgressed wantonly he is liable to Extirpation, and if in error to a Sin-offering; and if it was in doubt whether he had committed a transgression he is liable to a Suspensive Guilt-offering. (M.Ker. 1:2, Danby text, p. 563.)

Resh Lakish is reported to have said:

> Great is repentance, for because of it intentional sins are accounted as errors, as it is said: Return O Israel, unto the Lord, thy God; for thou hast stumbled in thy iniquity. Iniquity is premeditated, and yet he calls it stumbling. (Yoma 86b.)[14]

The same theme occurs in the Wisdom Literature. In Sirach 3:30 we are told that "almsgiving atones for sin," yet the reader is warned not to presume upon God's mercy or to "be so confident of atonement that you add sin to sin" or to avoid repentance because you assume that God's mercy is great (ch. 5:4–7). The limits of the sacrificial system are pointed to when the writer says:

> Do not commit a sin twice;
>   even for one you will not go unpunished.
> Do not say, "He will consider the multitude
>   of my gifts,
>   and when I make an offering to the Most High God he
>   will accept it."
>
> (Ch. 7:8–9.)

Later on in the same work the writer says that God does not accept the offerings that have been wrongfully obtained, and fasting for sins does no good if one does not refrain from committing those sins (ch. 34:18–26). He is especially sensitive to the danger of trying to bribe God and demonstrates strongly the position that keeping the law is the same as giving many offerings (ch. 35). Offerings are good and right in their place but have meaning especially when accompanied by repentance (ch. 38:9 f.). Forgiveness depends upon the attitude one takes toward his neighbor: "Forgive your neighbor the wrong he has done, and then your sins will be pardoned when you pray" (ch. 28:2). It is possible that the writer is attacking a concept of the atonement known as magical or objective. Only faint traces of such a view appear in the Jewish literature, although a clear example is found in II Macc. 3:31–40.

The stress on repentance and atonement is found also in the Qumran literature. Likewise, the Rabbinical traditions stress this aspect of forgiveness. In the tract Yoma, expression is given to it thus:

The sin-offering and the unconditional Guilt-offering effect atonement; death and the Day of Atonement effect atonement if there is repentance. Repentance effects atonement for lesser transgressions against both positive and negative commandments in the Law; while for graver transgressions it suspends punishment until the Day of Atonement comes and effects atonement. (Yoma 8:8.)

Here we see some gradations of the seriousness of sin and the ways in which repentance is evaluated. If repentance is present at death and the Day of Atonement effects atonement, it completely covers lesser transgressions, while for graver transgressions it suspends judgment. Yet man is warned not to presume upon God's grace. If a man deliberately decides to sin and repent and sin again and repent, "he will be given no chance to repent." If he sins with the assumption that the Day of Atonement will cover it, "the Day of Atonement effects no atonement." Furthermore, the Day of Atonement effects only the sins committed between God and man. Where sins exist between two people, one must first appease the other before the Day of Atonement is effective.

Repentance, then, is the key to forgiveness. God is ready to forgive, but man manifests his readiness to accept forgiveness by his turning about to face God. The Rabbinical writings especially abound in praise of repentance: Rabbi Jonathan said: "Great is repentance for it brings redemption"; Rabbi Chama b. Chanina: "Great is repentance for it brings healing into the world." R. Levi said: "Great is repentance, for it reaches up to the throne of glory." Rabbi R. Johannan said: "Great is repentance for it overrides a prohibition of the Torah," and Rabbi Meir used to say: "Great is repentance, for on account of an individual who repents, the sins of all the World are forgiven" (Yoma 86a and b).[15]

Thus once again John the Baptist appears a member in good standing of the Jewish community when he comes proclaiming "repentance unto the forgiveness of sins." He is the great transitional figure between Judaism and Christianity.

Before we leave our discussion of Judaism and turn to the New Testament, attention must be called to the most remarkable of all passages on forgiveness in Judaism. The Testament of Gad offers a striking passage which seems to bear close resemblance to the New Testament teaching on forgiveness. There is no need to argue for Christian influence here, although at other points in the

Testaments it is clearly evident. A stronger case can perhaps be made for some connection between the type of piety evident here and the Qumran group.

And now, my children, I exhort you, love ye each one his brother, and put away hatred from your hearts, love one another in deed, and in word, and in the inclination of the soul. For in the presence of my father I spake peaceably to Joseph; and when I had gone out, the spirit of hatred darkened my mind, and stirred up my soul to slay him. Love ye, therefore, one another from the heart; and if a man sin against thee, cast forth the poison of hate and speak peaceably to him, and in thy soul hold not guile; and if he confess and repent, forgive him. But if he deny it, do not get into a passion with him, lest catching the poison from thee he take to swearing and so thou sin doubly. . . . And if he be shameless and persist in his wrong-doing, even so forgive him from the heart, and leave to God the avenging. (Testament of Gad, ch. 6.)

From this passage it is clear that certain leaders in Judaism spoke of forgiveness not only as something that God in his grace bestows upon man. Forgiveness is also an experience between two fellowmen who have been separated because sin has come between them. It is proffered by one in order that sin may not increase. Love from the heart accompanies it, and the channel of exhortation or rebuke is used to make forgiveness operative. It may indeed be that we have here a "passage of truly epoch-making importance."[16] Although R. H. Charles exaggerates the contrast between the Old and New Testaments on this subject, he is probably right when he says: "These verses contain the most remarkable statement on the subject of forgiveness in all ancient literature."[17] They are keen in their analysis of human estrangement, although they solidly base forgiveness in God's love. The writer is not blindly optimistic about the outcome of such action, and counsels that if reconciliation is not possible, man can at least remove bitterness and hatred from his own life, and this can be done by "forgiving your brother from the heart." The relationship between human and divine forgiveness is seen here as intimately as in the New Testament. The whole subject is viewed from the standpoint of the dynamics of human relationships, even though it assumes that forgiveness can transcend the resources of human nature. God himself can supply strength to forgive.

Part Three

FORGIVENESS
IN THE NEW TESTAMENT

CHAPTER VII

The Forerunner: John the Baptist

John the Baptist has always been something of an enigma to readers of the New Testament. He appears on its earliest pages and deals with sin in the classical prophetic tradition by denouncing it with courage (Luke 3:19), even to those in places of high authority. Such denunciation, however, serves only one purpose: it aims to bring about repentance, which leads to confession, which in turn leads to forgiveness.

Although we have observed that the Old Testament is reluctant to talk about the accomplishment of forgiveness, focusing instead upon the anticipation of it in the future, Luke and Mark agree in using the phrase "the forgiveness of sins" in connection with John's ministry (Mark 1:4; Luke 3:3). John is that transitional person between the Old Covenant and the New who reiterates the same message of God's willingness to forgive, but this time the vague forward look is concretized in one person: "Behold the Lamb of God who takes away the sin of the world" (John 1:29). John's stress is on repentance and the public confession of sins, and the rite of baptism marks the beginning of a new life, which has a strict ethical quality. For the multitudes are urged to begin sharing food and clothing with the needy, the tax collectors are to be upright in their exactions, and the soldiers are to live by the standards laid upon them (Luke 3:10–14).

It is, of course, a difficult matter to separate the actual situation from the church's later interpretations of John's ministry. The modern reader of the New Testament, even when he has the ability to analyze the sources and remove some of the layers of interpretation, cannot be sure that his own bias and prejudice is not a great factor in evaluating degrees of primitiveness, etc. Furthermore, the desire to attain the *ipsissima verba* of Christ or to reconstruct the event "as it actually happened" belongs to a mentality different from that which motivates this study.

Seen from the perspective of what is known about first-century Judaism, the appearance of a man like John the Baptist on the scene is quite plausible. The political and religious ferment of first-century Palestine spawned not only revolutionaries but sectarians and quietists, some of whom arose like meteors and sank as quickly. When material like the Dead Sea Scrolls is discovered, only the ignorant assume that such a discovery discredits Christianity. Those who take the position that God works through history to accomplish his purposes will be confirmed in their position as they see the rich historical antecedents to Christianity in Jewish literary material.

What has become abundantly clear is that in the first century, the primary religious question of the Jew was: "How can I be at peace with God?" The Jew was concerned about forgiveness because he found the load of his sin unbearable. We have seen abundant evidence for this in the literary material of this period. It was precisely to this need that John the Baptist seems to have addressed himself most vigorously. With his call to repentance, we find a note reiterated that has been sounded already in the Old Testament, but the new element is his union of this call to a baptismal rite. This rite was neither "inherently efficacious" nor "merely symbolic." In Biblical thought the line between the symbol and the reality portrayed in it is so fragile that any discussion of the matter would have seemed to John to be quite beside the point. As a prophet, he rejects the idea that grace is transmitted by inheritance (Luke 3:8), yet he does not reject all cultic ceremonies. His baptism was "unto the forgiveness of sins," that is, pointing toward the forgiveness of sins, or even more strongly, offering the possibility of forgiveness of sins to people. (It is not as strong as Barnabas 11:1: "baptism that brings the remission of sins"; *to baptisma to pherōn aphesin hamartiōn.*) For the identical expression is used in the New Testament to refer to Christ's death: "This is my blood of the covenant, which is poured out for many for the forgiveness of sins" (Matt. 26:28). Peter calls upon his hearers to "repent, and be baptized every one of you in the name of Jesus Christ for the forgiveness of your sins; and you shall receive the gift of the Holy Spirit" (Acts 2:38).

There have been interpreters who have seen the meaning of *aphesis hamartiōn* to be "removal of sins" rather than remission or forgiveness of sins. According to this position, John is emphasizing not what God does in a forensic sense but what man does as he removes sin from his life. At the turn of the century Agnes Smith Lewis registered this opinion calling attention to the fact that the idea of forsaking is implied in the word *aphesis.* The

verb form is used of forsaking one's wife and even in
the New Testament is used for divorce (I Cor. 7:11). She
asks:

Is it quite impossible to read, "The baptism of repentance for
the forsaking of sins"? We have a strong suspicion that this
kind of *aphesis* was not altogether absent from the Baptist's
mind as he preached . . . . We may even presume to say that
the *aphesis* in the sense of forsaking is the only sure proof
that we have received the *aphesis* in the sense of acquittal.[1]

While Mrs. Lewis rejects too strongly any conception of
forgiveness being related to a ceremony like baptism,
and is rightly criticized for this by A. Carr in the same
journal, her point has not been lost.

Support for her interpretation comes from an article
by A. C. Deane some twenty years later. Like Mrs. Lewis,
he is aware of the ponderous precedents set by a scholarship which tends to assume that the expression means
"forgiveness of sins." Yet he too asks:

Are we quite certain that *aphesis* does, in this instance, mean
"forgiveness," i.e., remission by God? Literally of course, the
verb means to send away from one's self and this, its fixed
significance in classical Greek, is retained in the N. T. Is it not
at least possible that the substantive may bear sometimes a
sense cognate to this? Thus *aphesis hamartiōn* means literally
a "sending away" of sins . . . . There is no etymological reason
why it should not be used also to signify human effort, why, in
short, its true rendering here should not be "renunciation"—
sending away, by man rather than remission—putting away by
God.[2]

While Deane draws a sharp line between John's baptism
and that of the early church, his study suffers from an
overzealous attempt to keep divine forgiveness within the
context of the life of Jesus.

The idea that the primary meaning of forgiveness here is the laying aside of sins rather than divine pardon has been strongly championed recently by Harald Sahlin in his extensive studies of Lucan style. He agrees with Harnack that one does not expect the idea in the early sections of Luke that salvation consists in forgiveness, then proceeds:

Nor do I believe that to be the original meaning of the statement. What is involved here is not the forgiveness of sins on the part of God but the laying aside of sins on the part of man, putting aside one's sinful nature. Here we must not presuppose the later Christian idea of forgiveness of sins but the genuinely Jewish idea that the arrival of the Messiah includes a radical change of life on the part of the people who expect him. According to this point of view Luke 1:77 is clearly a unit: the Messiah will prepare "the ways of the Lord" by giving his people knowledge of salvation, so that they will lay aside their sins. The knowledge of salvation is the insight of right conduct pleasing unto God, the forgiveness of sins (*aphesis hamartiōn*) is the practical consequence of of this recognition: a radical break with the previous sinful nature. Taken together they constitute theoretical and practical repentance.

Sahlin bases his position not only on the meaning of the Greek, but most decisively on the proto-Lucan expression that lies at the basis of it. Luke, using a Hebrew original, took the well-known Christian expression, *aphesis hamartiōn*, to translate something that did not have that connotation. Indeed, the technical expression "forgiveness of sins" (*aphesis hamartiōn*) does not occur in the Greek Old Testament, and the word *aphesis* never occurs there with the meaning "forgiveness."[3] At no place in the Old Testament Greek is it used to translate the Hebrew word *salach*. Thus the original that Luke was translating was open to two translations: "so that he [the Messiah] will do away with their sins" or "so that they themselves may get rid of their sins." Since Judaism did not expect that the Messiah would do away with sin, Sahlin assumes that the original meaning of Luke 1:77 can only be: As man receives knowledge he will himself get rid of his sins and thus prepare the way for the coming of the Messiah.[4]

From this study of Luke 1:77 it would seem to be clear that the role of John the Baptist is defined consistently with the prophetic tradition. It is his responsiblity to "give knowledge of salvation to his people in the release from their sins."

When we look at the description of John's ministry, we find that two Gospel writers describe his work in terms of the formula, release from sins (Mark 1:4; Luke 3:3). Mark supplies another detail when he says that when men came to him they were openly confessing their sins (Mark 1:5; Matt. 3:6). The present tense of the verb would appear to stress the fact that such confession was not a singular event but repeated, and the preposition *ek* as part of the compound verb leaves us no other alternative but to assume that public confession of sins was a part of John's public services. In the genuine prophetic tradition, John proclaimed judgment if they did not heed his warning, and called for fruits of repentance.

It is, however, doubtful that he declared people forgiven. For one thing, all our sources indicate that he pointed people beyond himself to the One coming after him. There is no evidence, either, in the Gospels that he evoked any opposition from the leadership in Judaism.[5] Furthermore, we have already observed that Judaism did not expect the coming Messiah to forgive sins.

In John's case we seem to have instead a ritual that dramatically portrayed the washing away of sins. Just as removal of sins is suggested in Luke 1:77, it may be that here the forgiveness of sins means washing them away. God desires a holy and pure people, and according to Judaism, the coming of the Messiah was contingent upon that holiness. If only one Jew could perfectly keep the law, the Messiah would come.

John also seeks to bring about some preparation for the coming of the Messiah. In close parallel to Isa. 1:15 f., John admonishes his listeners to purify their ways and be cleansed so that they may be spared the judgment of Almighty God. So the baptism of John signifies in a dramatically real way that those who undergo it have said an emphatic no to their past, and as they repent in this way they commit themselves to serve God in the future. By doing so, they also become a part of a people, for it is a corporate experience, and the fact that we later read of John's disciples indicates that some religious bonds were formed through this experience. In fact, it is most likely that this was the major reason why Jesus joined the group of disciples around John. He too wanted to share in the Messianic Kingdom when it came, and perhaps he was himself most surprised that the role which he played was as great as it became.

There seems to be no reason, then, for accepting the verdict of Rudolf Otto that "with John the forgiveness of sins took place through a magical, sacramental rite of washing."[6] Indeed, such a position contradicts Josephus, who wrote that John's baptism was not used to beg off from sins committed. Carl Kraeling has taken the position that the words "for the forgiveness of sins" "describe not the action of the rite itself, but the action of God associated with the performance of the rite by man."[7] In Judaism at large, he says, no rite was ever produced that was efficacious in and of itself. Although John's baptism was not sacramental, it could still be associated with the forgiveness of sins.

The reason is that as an act of self-humiliation before God it was a clear, voluntary expression of true repentance, and that repentance was commonly acknowledged to have divine forgiveness as its response. If John's baptism, then, was an act of repentance it could mediate forgiveness without conferring it. It could mediate forgiveness without being a sacrifice.[8]

With the baptism of John, then, we are in the presence of an act that can only be described as an "innovation in the field of religious rite."[9]

Whatever may be the meaning of his baptism, it is clear that according to the writers of the Gospels, John served as a forerunner for Jesus Christ. Whether he explicitly assured people of the forgiveness of sin in the way that Jesus did is highly doubtful. Most likely he stopped short of that, since we have no evidence that the Jewish leaders rejected the ministry of John (Matt. 21:23–27; Mark 11:27–33; Luke 20:1–8) with anything like the firmness they displayed toward Jesus.

It is probably most correct to see John in the procession of Old Testament prophets who called for repentance and for evidence that this repentance had taken place through baptism and restitution. Such a preacher would certainly have no trouble gathering about himself many adherents. On the other hand, it is only logical to assume that there were those who did not accept John's modesty and sought to make more of him than he had claimed, perhaps because they shared John's uncertainty about Jesus when the ministry of Christ did not follow along the lines of his expectation (Matt. 11:2–30; Luke 7:18–35). Jesus himself paid elaborate tribute to John, calling him "the greatest born of woman" (Matt. 11:11) and "the Elijah who is

to come" (v. 14). According to John 1:21,25, John dis-
claimed this title, and although we may admit that the
interests of the early church played a significant role in the
selection of this material, is it not possible to assume that
the Fourth Gospel is correctly reflecting the modesty of
John the Baptist? The other elements of our picture of
John the Baptist would harmonize with such a position.[10]

Thus, John the Baptist stands between two worlds: the
world in which forgiveness is promised and the world of
the New Covenant in which forgiveness is realized. From
the world of the Old Covenant he brings the importance
of the confession of sins and makes it more explicit than
it had ever been under the Old Covenant (note the word
exomologeō—used for public confession of sins, Matt. 3:6;
Mark 1:5). But beyond the Old Covenant he also points
explicitly to the one who has finally come and who bears
(removes) the sin of the world (John 1:29). In this statement, the writer of the Fourth Gospel sees more than
John the Baptist put into it, but there is no doubt that
the portrait of John the Baptist offered to us in the Fourth
Gospel is essentially reliable.[11]

The place of John the Baptist is highlighted by his use
of baptism as a seal to commitment that it had not pre-
viously had. His ministry became an integral part of the
earliest kerygma (Acts 10:37), because he united within
himself the Old and the New and was the first seriously
and openly to challenge the religious security of his contemporaries (Luke 3:7-9). The ministry of Jesus Christ
attached itself to John's, but with the baptism of Jesus the
mission of John the Baptist was completed.[12]

CHAPTER VIII

Jesus and the Forgiveness of Sins

From the earliest times, the church affirmed that Jesus had dealt decisively with the sin question. It comes to expression in the name Jesus itself, which Matthew tells us was chosen: "because he will save his people from their sins" (Matt. 1:21). Thus, Matthew uses the familiar words from Ps. 130:8 to apply to the ministry of Jesus, asserting that in him this great anticipation of the Jewish people has arrived. Although Judaism saw the Messianic Age as one in which sin would no longer be a factor of human existence, Judaism did not assert that the Messiah would forgive sins or deal with it in the way that the New Testament describes. For when Matthew uses the word "save" he is thinking of more than merely "rescue" or "deliver." To save a people from sin meant to deliver them from its bondage and also from its ravages as well. The meaning of the term is to restore a wholeness that has been lost. In the psalm that Matthew quotes we find the writer anxiously asking who will bring salvation to his people and who will save them from their sins. The writer urges his people to wait for the Lord. Matthew believes that the longing of the psalmist (Ps. 130) has been answered in Jesus. To fear the Lord is to wait for his word of forgiveness and expect deliverance only from him.[1]

The forgiveness of sins or deliverance from them is the inclusive way of describing the total salvation of God in both Old and New Testaments. To forgive is to remove not only the debt but also the barrier that has been placed between God and man. To "save" from sins means to "help," and to offer wholeness, which comes as a result of God's presence among his people.[2] Thus Matt. 1:21 describes the sending of the Son of Man in similar terms to those found in Mark 2:10. Ernst Lohmeyer comments in this connection:

Eschatological fulfilment here is so closely bound up with saving from sin that all other hopes contained in the Jewish faith —hopes for peace and dominion, for the unity and indestructibility of the Jewish people, and all other expressions of religio-nationalistic expectation—vanish like a puff of earthly smoke before the heavenly light of forgiveness of sin.[3]

To deal with sin must not, however, simply be equated with the forgiving of sins. The forgiving of sins may after all be only one way in which sin is dealt with. When we analyze the New Testament terminology dealing with forgiveness, we observe first that the verb *aphiēmi* occurs twenty times in connection with the noun "sins." It occurs an additional seven times with "debts" (or cognates) as its object, and once with the noun "trespass" as its object. It must be admitted that this is a surprisingly small number of occurrences. The expression "forgiveness of sins" (*aphesis hamartiōn*) occurs only eleven times in the whole New Testament, with *aphesis paraptōmata* once (Eph. 1:7) and the absolute usage of the word "forgiveness" occurring an additional three times. It should be observed further that Luke is responsible for seventeen of the total number of usages and that he has the technical expression "forgiveness of sins" a total of eight times, whereas it occurs only once in Matthew and Mark and only once in the Pauline literature (Col. 1:14), although Ephesians has a related form "forgiveness of trespasses" (Eph. 1:7).

Having briefly looked at the total New Testament usage, we are ready to examine the way in which the Gospel writers viewed Jesus' work.

THE HEALING OF THE PARALYTIC

The three Synoptic Gospels describe the healing of the paralytic in some detail. There are a goodly number of agreements between Matthew and Luke in their accounts and enough common material to suggest the possibility of dependence upon Mark by Matthew and Luke. Yet each writer has his distinctive approach. In each Gospel the narrative has its peculiar place and therefore makes its own contribution to the total story of Jesus.

We have noted that the word for "forgiveness" (both verb and noun forms) occurs some thirty-eight times in the New Testament. Altogether it occurs eleven times in the accounts of this incident, always in the verb form (Matt., three times; Mark, four times; Luke, four times). It would seem best from a methodological point of view to examine each narrative in its setting. We begin with Mark, since it is commonly held that he is our earliest Gospel writer.

Mark 2:1–12

The story is identical in its major outlines in all three Gospels. A man comes, against obstacles, to be healed of a paralytic condition. All writers agree in telling us that the faith of the ones bearing him and of the paralyzed man made Jesus look with favor upon his need. In Mark and Matthew, Jesus addresses him with the word "Child" (*Teknon*). The word connotes tenderness and endearment. The rest of that sentence is, however, a surprise. The man has come for healing; instead, Jesus declares him forgiven. It is futile to speculate that the man had guilt written all over his face or to attempt to psychologize the incident. As William Wrede remarked, it is not likely that Mark assumed that the paralytic was a normal Lutheran Christian.[4]

Nevertheless, the introduction of the idea of sin and forgiveness in this narrative has caused a good deal of trouble for modern interpreters. Ever since 1904, when Wrede published an article on this material, it has become increasingly popular to assume that Mark 2:5b–10 (incl.) are an insertion that does not really belong here. Although Wrede called it "a growth" (*ein Zuwachs*),[5] Lohmeyer called it a "dogmatic insertion" that could hardly belong to the original story.[6] The technical aspects of this problem cannot detain us here.[7] Already the form critics, however, were not agreed on the structure of this pericope. Martin Dibelius differed with Bultmann and felt that in this case we can detect "a change and a trimming but not a complete inversion of the actual event" and arrives at this conclusion on the basis of the quite "unchristological" ending. He rejects Bultmann's theory that the Palestinian church used this to prove its right to forgive sins by its power to heal by miracle because "it is very doubtful whether there were any discussions of this kind in the Christian church in the years A.D. 50–70."[8]

In view of the intrinsic structure of the pericope and the fact that the twelve objections to the unity that Mead has listed do not find an adequate answer in the solutions proposed, it would seem best to assume that we have here a literary unit. It certainly may be the case "that inferential value judgments about the so-called pronouncement section have had as much, if not more, to do with the combination hypothesis as have formal criteria."[9]

Why, then, does Jesus deal with the sins of this man when he comes asking for healing? Because he accepts the Jewish point of view that there is a relation between healing and forgiveness, between sin and sickness. Mead is certainly correct when he says that "the premise that sickness connects with sin is neither affirmed nor denied; it is *used*."[10] Wrede, also, has already noted that there is no evidence to indicate that this man had been a particularly bad sinner; rather, at the basis of the narrative lies the belief that sickness derives ultimately from sin.[11]

It would be misleading to assert that Jesus never relates sin and sickness. He warns, to be sure, that when accidents happen we are not to assume that we are better than those who were hurt (Luke, ch. 13), and in the case of the man born blind the question of who sinned is brushed aside as an irrelevant one on that occasion (John, ch. 9). Yet the lame man healed at the pool of Bethesda is warned to go and sin no more so that a worse fate may not befall him (John 5:14). We can only deduce that Jesus saw a relationship between sin and sickness and that in the case of the paralytic he addressed himself first to that need which was greatest in his mind.

The direct address: "Child, your sins are being forgiven," is such a departure from traditional practices that it evoked the immediate response of the Jews who were present. They could only call it blasphemy. The priests were, of course, commissioned to declare God's forgiveness to the people as a people but they were not commissioned to do so to a specific individual. Personal forgiveness always remained an open question, and whoever claimed that he could answer it was guilty of putting himself in the place of God, hence, guilty of blasphemy. "Who is able to forgive sins, except one, God?" The thoughts they have are recorded as unexpressed, but Jesus is aware of their nature, nonetheless. This does not assume any mental telepathy or clairvoyance; it merely assumes a knowledge of the way that the Pharisaic mind works. Jesus addresses himself to their question by asking them which they consider easier: To say to the paralytic, "Your sins are forgiven" or to say, "Rise, take up your bed and walk"? From one point of view it would seem that it is easier to say, "Your sins are forgiven," for no one can tell whether they are or not. To say, "Take up your bed and walk," knowing full well that the man cannot walk, is either taunting him or if he should get up and walk, doing something unusual but not unheard of. Jesus actually never says which is hardest, and any attempt on our part to answer his question must be preliminary, since there are a number of perspectives from which the question can be asked and answered.

With Mark 2:10, however, we come to the main point of the narrative. The question is, in fact, raised only to prepare for Jesus' affirmation that in order for them to know that the Son of Man has authority to forgive sins on earth, he commands the paralytic, "I say to you, rise." It is quite possible that Mark has editorial additions here. We find it hard to conceive that Jesus would have called himself "Son of Man" to his opponents this early in his ministry, and even harder to suppose that they would recognize that he was referring to himself. On the other hand, the term "Son of Man" was his favorite way of avoiding the use of the personal pronoun, and it seems equally difficult to assume that Jesus in fact said: "That you may see that I have authority to ..."

Two other matters seem to be more significant. The reference to authority (*exousia*) occurs in all three Gospels and is important not only here but throughout the life of Christ. Already in Mark 1:27 attention is called to the fact that Christ acts with authority. What is really meant by this reference to authority? Clearly our pericope deals with this subject from the standpoint of forgiveness. For it is in his declaration of forgiveness to the individual that the outer limits of the authority of Jesus are decided. As Hans von Campenhausen has said:

As he forgives sin, Jesus sets himself not only against the law which is still in force, indeed still demands the punishment of the sinner, but steps forward directly to a place reserved by Judaism only for God. . . . Jesus himself does not need any so-called justification of his authority especially since it is justified or demonstrated through his deed. Thus the people do not praise him, but God who has given such fullness of authority to man . . . . This double aspect, the eternal and the extraordinary, that which was valid from the beginning and that which is unique permeates the total proclamation of Jesus and describes the secret of his person. It cannot be removed by distributing the references among the various layers of tradition . . . . Jesus had no office, but he had a commission and he is at the same time the one sent, who from the beginning and from within corresponds to his commission.

He does not need like the rest of the prophets to receive the spirit of God or his gift, for he stands entirely upon the side of God. Nor is he an office-bearer in any usual sense, he does not appeal to his commission; for commission and office coincide in his person.[12]

What we have said is that in Christ an unusual authority existed; authority and person coincided perfectly, and in this case it was expressed through the fact that he spoke the word of forgiveness.

A second feature that needs to be stressed involves the words, "upon the earth" (ch. 2:10). The forgiveness of sins takes place not in a heavenly decree or by a resolution that God makes in the beyond. It is on earth that the forgiving takes place, and this merely adds to the scandal of the assertion. Forgiving sins does not threaten us as long as it remains God's prerogative in the holiness of heaven. But when it is brought down into the raw immediacy of life upon earth, that is a different matter. The proof that the man has been forgiven is furnished by the fact that he stands up and walks. To the people asking for a sign, none was given, yet to those who had faith, signs came in again and again to confirm and strengthen the faith that was theirs. The signs of health and forgiveness came as evidence that God's power was available to them, and that he came not to see men crippled by sin but to see them walk upright and forgiven of their sins.

The Marcan ending is not taken up by either Luke or Matthew. Although all three say that all the people glorified God, only Mark adds: "We never saw anything like this!" In the total structure of Mark, it is important to note that the complaint is made immediately after this account that Jesus eats with sinners (v. 16). Little wonder, for the people were not able to comprehend how Jesus could be so free to meet with sinners. They had tried separation from them, and this seemed to be the best solution Judaism had toward sin. But Jesus by his approach shows that forgiveness no longer makes one afraid to meet and eat with sinners, because one has something to offer them that is better than sharing their dilemma.

Matthew 9:1–8

Several interesting differences appear between Matthew's account and those of Mark and Luke. Matthew alone places the healing by the wayside. Although Matthew also has Jesus addressing the man as child, he adds the further word, "Take heart" (*Tharsei*), which occurs twice in Mark (ch. 6:50; 10:49) and three times in the Gospel of Matthew (ch. 9:2,22; 14:27).

The Matthean addition *Tharsei*, variously translated as "Take heart" or "Take courage," occurs only rarely in the New Testament, but when it does, it conveys a significant point. Walter Grundmann has shown that the same word is important in the Platonic dialogue, *Phaedo*, where the discussion revolves about the possibility of courage in the face of death. Courage there is grounded in the knowledge of the immortality of the soul.[13]

Over against this, the word is found in the New Testament predominantly on the lips of Jesus or spoken by someone who is convinced that God will act on their behalf in the concrete historical situation in which they find themselves. "Always," Grundmann says, "men are admonished to take courage in view of what Jesus gives to them and is to them."[14] In this context, in Matthew it is clear that the paralytic's reason to take courage is that the sin question has finally received hope of solution. He is not pointed to some vague future date when his sin will be forgiven or to some distant tribunal when he will be acquitted. Forgiveness is assured him here and now, and when that happens, ground for courage appears. Jesus acts in history; he does not merely speak promises for the beyond.[15]

In Matthew's Gospel this narrative is placed in the context of Jesus' attack against sickness, demon possession, and death. Adolf Schlatter comments that Jesus could not have helped the sick, etc., had he not had the power also to forgive sins. It is, however, precisely at this point that the conflict arises between Jesus and Jewish piety, and according to Schlatter, with all branches of Jewish piety, including the scribes, the Pharisees, the disciples of John. Because he brings the grace of God, he becomes a riddle to all of these groups. Their resistance to him had a serious basis. In freeing himself from every restriction in his friendship toward sinners, Jesus placed himself above the law and represented the omnipotence of creative grace. In this act all the others saw the shaking of the foundations that they had labored so diligently to build up.[16]

Another significant change found in Matthew is the conclusion. He alone says: "And they gave glory to God, who had given such great authority to men." The reference to authority and the plural *men* have provoked a number of comments. Schlatter saw the plural as evidence of Matthew's conviction that the omnipotence of Jesus to forgive sins became a possession of the church, and he calls our attention to Matt. 16:19 and 18:18.[17] Rudolf Bultmann has followed Schlatter in this point and argues that "Mark 2 has been given its place because the Church wanted to trace back to Jesus *its* own right to forgive sins."[18] We shall defer to a later time a discussion about the plausibility of Jesus' making a declaration of forgiveness.

Luke 5:17–26

The only difference of any importance in Luke's account is the tense of the verb *aphiēmi* in v. 20. Although both Mark and Matthew have the present tense, Luke has the Doric aorist. This would mean that the process of the forgiving of sins has been completed. According to both Matthew and Mark, the forgiving of sins is just now beginning, thus providing hope that the paralytic will eventually arrive at the full forgiveness of his sins, whereas the Lucan statement would assure him that the process has already been completed.

THE WOMAN WHO WAS A SINNER

The narrative of the sinful woman recorded only by Luke is of great importance for the topic of forgiveness, since it is the only other place in the Gospel tradition where the direct assertion: "Your sins are forgiven" occurs. Within the Lucan narrative it is evident that it is designed to serve as an illustration of the manner in which Jesus dealt with sinners, for it is set in the context of the statement: "The Son of Man arrived eating and drinking wine, a friend of tax collectors and sinners" (ch. 7:34).

The setting is a feast or at least a banquet meal prepared at the home of a Pharisee. The words "and behold" (*kai idou*), which open v. 37, indicate the element of surprise at the entry of a woman "who was in the city a sinner." The relative pronoun used in the Greek to introduce the description of the woman lays especial emphasis on the kind of character she was. The stress on her sinfulness appears three times. The Pharisee is especially shocked by the fact that such a woman would be permitted to "touch" Jesus (v. 39). Luke does not allow us the option of assuming that Jesus did not know about the true nature of this woman, for Jesus himself says to Simon: "Her sins, which are many, are forgiven" (v. 47).

Since there are some similarities between this account and the various other anointings described in the Gospels, efforts have been made to show that this is merely a recasting of the last anointing and that it serves especially to underline Luke's interest in forgiveness.[19] Here is a perfect example of a sin-oppressed soul finding forgiveness in the presence of Christ. A strong case can indeed be made for this position.

There is, however, another possibility that deserves closer study. It is possible that Luke had access to two accounts of an anointing and that he preferred this one because it fitted better into the way he viewed the ministry of Jesus. The narrative as it stands in Luke is a masterpiece of psychological description, and there is no reason on internal grounds to deny its genuineness. Every action is plausible; none bears the mark of invention or fabrication. The editorial hand of Luke is apparent, but this is precisely what one would expect.

The narrative centers on two types: the self-righteous one who needs no forgiveness and the type that is overwhelmed by its own unworthiness and sinfulness. The woman's intention, apparently, was to give Christ a token of her love and gratitude, and it took effort on her part (v. 37) to find where he was and to seek him out. She belonged to the "sinner" type. The Pharisee's mind is keenly aware of the types and knows that only the foolish or the wicked ignore these boundary lines. For a moment he is ready to consign Jesus to the group of the ignorant. The woman's simple act cannot be carried out because she has an emotional breakdown before she can complete it. After that, she merely acts hastily from one embarrassing moment to another. The Pharisee feels that Jesus is becoming a participant in sin by allowing himself to be "touched" by this woman. Contact with sin means defilement.

The parable, however, sorts out another dimension of Simon's thought that interests Jesus even more. The point of the parable seems to be that a saint is one whose life is motivated by gratitude. The woman sensed her sin keenly, was deeply grateful for the amount of her debt that had been canceled, and expressed this gratitude in the only way she knew. Ointment that may earlier have been used to further her trade was now used to anoint Christ. It is rather manifest that she did not come merely as a penitent to bemoan her guilt. She had already repented and begun a new life and was now expressing her gratitude to Christ.

Yet there are indications in the text that argue against the assertion that she had already received forgiveness. For one thing, the word of the Pharisee in v. 39 militates against it, and the narrator does not indicate that the Pharisee is mistaken. Also, the explicit word of forgiveness spoken to the woman and the final word, "Depart in peace," would argue for a first encounter.

Hans Windisch concludes that it was only during this encounter with Jesus that she actually received the forgiveness of sins and the release from her conscience.[20] The unity of the narrative can only be safeguarded if we assume that the certain hope that her contrition had been accepted drove her to Jesus and compelled her to do her work. No doubt she also sought confirmation of this certainty. This personal encounter with Jesus brought her to an experience of full forgiveness. Windisch sees here the explanation of the mutual relationship of forgiveness of sins and proof of love.

Forgiveness of sins bears fruit in works of love and works of love call forth or testify to the full revelation of the former. The narrative then shows us something of the impression made by the Savior upon sensitive spirits and of the working of his act of salvation.[21]

In conclusion, it may be said that in spite of the problems in this narrative, its major focus is clear. For the opponent of Jesus, it raises the question of his identity. If he were really a prophet, he would not allow the sinner to touch him. Luke 7:36–38 contains the exposition, without expressly formulating the problem, while vs. 44–46 and 48 f. answer the question thus: Jesus does not condone sin in relating himself to the sinner but, rather, sees the sin as forgiven (v. 47) or actually forgives it (v. 48). "The point of the story accordingly is this: Jesus does not separate himself from the sinners; which means that he forgives sin, not that he approves of sin."[22]

SIMON PETER

Accounts of Jesus' dealing directly with sinners do not actually abound in great numbers in the Gospels. Windisch has observed that their number is relatively small as compared to the healing and controversy narratives.[23] They are: the call of Simon Peter (Luke 5:1–11); the healing of the paralytic (Mark 2:1–12 and parallels); the sinner in the house of Simon (Luke 7:35–50); the adulterous woman in the apocryphal addition of John 8:1–11; Jesus' visit with Zacchaeus (Luke 19:1–10); the denial of Peter recorded in Luke 22:31 ff., 61; and finally, Jesus' discussion with the thief on the cross (Luke 23:39–43). Furthermore, only Luke has the parable of the two men going to the Temple to pray, in which the prayer, "God be merciful to me a sinner," occurs. Of all the stories dealing with sinners directly, then, only the paralytic and the adulterous woman occur in other Gospels in addition to, or in place of, Luke. The striking thing is Luke's interest in this side of Jesus' mission. Since it bears directly on forgiveness, we may look at each of these incidents in our efforts to arrive at Luke's view of forgiveness.[24]

The first instance in which a person describes himself as sinful in the presence of Christ is recorded by Luke 5:1–11. Although the call of the four is also recorded by Matthew and Mark, Luke alone describes Peter's reaction to the great catch of fish in the words: "Depart from me, I am a sinner, Lord" (v. 8). What brought him to this confession? Certainly no lengthy sermon on what a poor fisherman Peter was or what a wicked person he was! From the narrative it is clear that Peter is brought to an awareness of sins through the great power of Jesus Christ. He has already gained respect for him by listening to him teach to the extent that he can say, "Sir, through the whole night we labored and caught nothing, but at your word I will let out the nets" (v. 5). The word used for "Lord" here is not the same as in v. 8, where the word *kurios* occurs.

Jesus does not meet Peter's confession here with a word of forgiveness. Instead, he encourages him not to fear and gives him a new commission for his life (v. 10). Perhaps his lack of self-esteem is removed by the new and greater task assigned to him by Jesus. As Peter becomes a fisher of men, at least he will find power to overcome his own sense of sin as he spends his life rescuing others from its bondage. The main element in Peter's consciousness of sin is the miracle and the impression made by the one who performed it. Being close to the power and holiness of this man brought Peter to an awareness of his own state. Fear is his response. In the case of Isaiah (ch. 6:7), and of Zechariah in Luke (ch. 1:13), words of assurance came after the experience of fear. Here there is no assurance of pardon, merely a commission. Thus the central point of this narrative seems to be the commission to apostleship. The consciousness of sin serves as a subsidiary motif.

During the passion week Luke alone records the warning that Jesus gives to Peter that Satan will try to sift him but that he has prayed for him. Here again the commission is given: "When you have repented, strengthen the brethren" (ch. 22:31–32). Peter did betray his Lord, after which Luke tells us, "The Lord turned and looked upon

Peter" (v. 61), and Peter remembered the warning and went out and wept bitterly. It is a remarkable tribute to the early church that it never held this betrayal against Peter. The raw material used to build the church consists, not of perfect people, but of people who are sensitive to their failures and who have the capacity to weep over their sins. For such forgiveness is always available, and to such the commission is given: "Feed my lambs" and "Strengthen the brethren."

ZACCHAEUS

The story of Zacchaeus fits into this category as well, because the crowd murmurs that Jesus invites himself into the house of Zacchaeus. Luke, who again is the only writer to report the incident, records the crowd as saying: "By a sinful man he has entered to rest" (Luke 19:7). Earlier we have been told that he is a wealthy man, and his response to the presence of Jesus as contrasted to Peter's was one of joy and eager anticipation. Nor are we told how Zacchaeus looked upon his own life. The closest that he comes to making a confession is to say: "If I have defrauded any one of anything, I restore it fourfold" (v. 8). One might argue that the *ei* clause with the indicative in the original indicates that he is making a confession, since this could well be translated: "Where I have defrauded . . ." What is remarkable about this incident is that no evidence of remorse is given beyond the clear resolution to change his ways. We may surely gather from the story that his wealth was illegitimately gained, so that after this encounter with Jesus he is immediately ready to give half of it to the poor. From the remaining half he will repay fourfold those who have been victims of his fraudulent acts.

Jesus replies that salvation has come to this house today, that he is a true son of Abraham, and he concludes with the general statement: "For the son of man has come to seek and to save the lost" (v. 10). From the man himself we have no direct confession of sin but, rather, a clearly stated intention to change his ways. Jesus considers him lost; the crowds considered him a sinner. The narrative indicates again the great power of direct contact with sinners and introduces the note of restitution. We may note in passing that Zacchaeus offers restitution; it is not required of him by Jesus. The fact that this is the only place in Biblical literature where the note of restitution is introduced is worth recording. Its implications for our view of the dynamics of Christian forgiveness will be discussed later.

Luke especially stresses the power of this kind of interaction with sinners. The moving parables of ch. 15, which are used by Matthew as examples of church discipline, are used by Luke to invite the murmuring ones to join in rejoicing because the one coin, sheep, and son has returned. In ch. 7 Jesus still had to justify his approach of dealing thus with sinners. By now apparently the Pharisees knew that people changed when Jesus dealt thus with them. But they could not yet rejoice with him, and the parables in ch. 15 constitute an invitation to join with the angels in rejoicing that some who have left the fold have again returned because of the diligence of the shepherd, the housewife, and the father.

The Criminal on the Cross

All four Gospels tell us that even in Christ's last hours on the cross he was in the company of the people he had been closest to all his life—the sinners. Luke gives us the fullest details about the response of the criminals who died with him. The one reviled, with similar words to those used by the soldiers: "Are you not the Christ? Save yourself and us!" (ch. 23:39). He apparently hoped to profit from his association with Christ, yet the tone of his statement led the other criminal to rebuke him with the words:

Do you not fear God, since you are under the same sentence of condemnation? And we indeed justly; for we are receiving the due reward of our deeds; but this man has done nothing wrong. (Vs. 40–41.)

If Mark and Matthew are correct in indicating that *both* criminals reviled Jesus at the beginning, then this would mean that the one criminal was changed by this brief encounter with Jesus on the cross, perhaps by the prayer of Jesus for his enemies. At any rate he now asks, "Jesus, remember me when you come in your kingly power" (v. 42). This prayer represents one of the most elemental requests, and it is significant, since it is rewarded with the promise that he will be in Paradise with Christ. The charter member of the church is a thief on the cross who takes his last gamble with Jesus and his Kingdom. The elemental request to be remembered by Jesus, this one expression of interest and loyalty to Christ, could not remain unanswered even in that dark hour. The focus is not on guilt, although the criminal recognizes his guilt. Jesus does not declare him forgiven, although surely we may judge that the implication of his statement is forgiveness. He grants him the assurance that they will not be separated even by death. Thus, as the first major miracle recorded in the Gospels assures a paralytic of forgiveness, so the last act that Jesus performs for a human being is to give assurance to a criminal that he will not be separated from someone who, he feels, "has done nothing wrong."

Luke has a particular interest in the sin question and in the subject of forgiveness. Yet there is no developed psychology of conversion. The message that comes to man reveals him in his situation, informs him of the coming judgment, and reveals the fact that he is a sinner. No demonstration of man's sinfulness occurs in the preaching. The idea of sin, in fact, occurs only in connection with the declaration of forgiveness and lacks all cosmological or speculative features. It is a possibility for all, but for Luke it is clear that not all need forgiveness, for there are those who are obviously living within the scope of the law.[25] For those who are sick or lost, Luke describes the content of salvation as "life" or "wholeness." The basis for this life is forgiveness, which in turn is conditional upon repentance.[26]

THE WOMAN CAUGHT IN THE ACT OF ADULTERY

There is little indeed about forgiveness in the Fourth Gospel. The story of the woman of Samaria certainly does not focus on the question of guilt and release from it, although something resembling a conversion is obviously recorded. The story of the adulterous woman does not belong in the area of Johannine literature, yet for the sake of convenience we will treat it here, since English Bibles traditionally placed it in the Gospel of John.

There is unanimous agreement among knowledgeable scholars that the pericope dealing with the adulterous woman could not have been written by the same man who wrote the rest of the Fourth Gospel. Its style is so different that this is simply not possible. The continuity of the narrative remains intact when we do not insert the words between John 7:52 and ch. 8:12, thus giving strong support to the position that the words were not originally in the Johannine text. We note also that the earliest manuscripts of the Fourth Gospel do not contain this story; indeed, it appears in no manuscript prior to the third century.

The reliability of the story is not now under discussion. This is clearly another matter and should not be confused with the textual problem. The fact that Papias, of about A.D. 125, shows awareness of the incident indicates that it may have circulated as a Gospel fragment as early as A.D. 100. In the second century there were those who advocated its use, and thus it began to appear in Christian sources toward the end of the second century. No doubt the fact that adultery arose as a problem in the church contributed to the popularity of the story, and it was used by those who argued that Jesus would have taken a "forgiving" approach to people ensnarled in such a sin.

To say that the story was used much in the second and third centuries, however, is not the same as to say that it was born out of the controversy. This seems on linguistic and other grounds improbable. There is no evidence that the controversy about dealing with adultery was severe by A.D. 100, nor is there any indication that the church simply produced stories to meet their problems. It seems more consistent with the historical evidence to conclude that the Palestinian churches preserved this pericope for the church, and from internal grounds we see no reason to assume that it could not have taken place very much as it is described in our most reliable texts.[27]

The incident is well known. While Jesus is teaching, the leaders bring him a woman who has been caught in the very act of adultery. The evidence thus is clear, and their only purpose in bringing her to his attention is to have his opinion on whether or not she ought to be stoned as the law requires. His past record in dealing with people like her was such that they had reason to believe he would "be soft on sin," and if he openly recommended a lenient approach, then they could naturally accuse him of minimizing or disparaging the law, for which the penalty was grave. Perhaps, on the other hand, if he would advocate the death penalty, they might have charged him with the usurpation of an authority that belonged only to Rome. Whatever may have been the exact horns of the dilemma on which they sought to impale him, it is clear that he does not even as much as nibble at their bait.

The response of Jesus must be read from the content of what he wrote on the ground and what he said. Derrett has presented a convincing argument for the position that the first time Jesus stooped down to write on the ground he wrote the words from Ex. 23:1: "You shall not join hands with a wicked man, to be a malicious witness."[28] The reasons why Jesus wrote this are given in detail. The words "caught in the very act" point not only to observation of actual intercourse on the part of at least two witnesses but also point strongly in the direction of a plot most likely engineered by the husband of the woman. Thus all the witnesses were a part of a conspiracy to bring the woman to this kind of justice, but they refused to obey that part of the law which asserts that every Israelite has an obligation to prevent a fellow Israelite from sinning whenever possible. The sin of the witnesses consists in not attempting to prevent what might easily have been prevented.[29]

The crowd was not satisfied with what Jesus wrote, although they probably understood its meaning clearly. At any rate, his oral statement made it explicit that he ex-

pected the innocent one to cast the first stone. Since it was
the responsibility of the witness to cast the first stone and
since it was obvious that the witnesses incurred guilt by
their failure to interrupt a sin they saw being committed,
no one could begin throwing stones. They would be joining hands with the wicked if they stoned her when her
guilt was not firmly established. In the meantime Jesus
stooped to write again; Derrett feels that this time Jesus
wrote Ex. 23:7 to round off his opinion: "From a false
matter keep far, and the innocent and righteous slay not;
for I shall not acquit the guilty." It was on this text that
the rabbis later hung the rules that one should not associ-
ate with a sinner as cojudge or cowitness. Since the second
witness is invariably the younger man, the responsibility
to guarantee the probity of the elder witness falls upon
him. Should the elder witness be disqualified, the younger
becomes guilty of the sin of association with the wicked,
and the total testimony falls to the ground. Derrett says:

When the older men reflect upon this position the implications
are uncomfortable. Their zealous juniors are entitled to inquire into every type of sin . . . . What of the sin of standing
by and not preventing the sin of one's brother? There is a
positive obligation to rebuke and to prevent a brother's sin;
and from many sins (some of which had a sexual character) a
Jew might lawfully be saved even at the cost of his life.[30]

Whatever may be the exact situation, and it appears that
Derrett has an unusually strong case, we must be clear that
the action of Jesus is not to be equated with forgiveness.
He stands with the woman at the center of the circle of
condemnation, and at that hour he is the only friend she
has. His refusal to condemn her does not mean that he
tolerates what she has done. He calls her action a sin and
bids her desist from it; yet he does so *after* he has shown

her that he is *for* her and not against her. His judgment, obliquely spoken, has greatest promise of being heeded and bearing redemption because a relationship has already been established between the two of them that can carry the freight of such judgment.

From the standpoint of the dynamics of human experience, it is clear that Jesus identified with both the law and the sinner. Basically, of course, the law, too, is always for the sinner. It is meant to protect him from hurting society and himself. Laws that do not are not just. The woman had, perhaps for the first time in her life, found a man who did not offer her counterfeit love and who had no desire to use her to his own ends or to destroy her. Such an encounter was the strongest resource imaginable for the gentle command that dismissed her: "Go and sin no more."

THE WORD FROM THE CROSS

The word from the cross (Luke 23:34),[31] "Father, forgive them, for they know not what they do," is recorded only by Luke, and the textual support for it is rather evenly divided. Marcion, of the second century, and Origen, of the third, have it, while the Syriac versions are divided. Codex D,* which tends to have the longer readings, does not have this one. If it was not spoken by Jesus and was not an original part of Luke's Gospel, how did it become a part of the Gospel tradition? Would the idea that the crucifixion was such a heinous crime that it could not be forgiven have been the motive for deleting it? From a theological point of view it can be pointed out that had Jesus not said this word from the cross, we would still have to say that his whole life was an expression of God's willingness to forgive his enemies.

For whom is the request made? For the Jews or for the Gentiles? Luke does not stress the responsibility of Rome in the crucifixion, but it may be that he is here thinking of the Romans, since at other points Gentiles and ignorance are related to each other. If it applies to the Jews, it can only mean that they are ignorant about the magnitude of their crime, since Luke portrays them as quite aware of the claims made by Jesus. The position taken by Adolf Schlatter that the prayer is meant for those who have placed Jesus between two criminals does not seem to express what is really involved here. Rather, the prayer is spoken on behalf of the executioners and those responsible for the execution more indirectly. Any effort to pinpoint the blame for the crucifixion should take seriously this request for forgiveness for the guilty ones.

We should observe that this is not a statement forgiving them. Not even Christ can forgive his enemies and persecutors. What he does is intercede on their behalf before God. He prays that they may eventually come to experience God's forgiveness. On the cross the greatest barrier of all is removed. In Christ, bitterness toward our destroyers can be overcome as we intercede on their behalf. We can pray that they may experience forgiveness, even when we cannot forgive them, because they neither ask for forgiveness nor know that they need it.

On the basis of the evidence we have looked at, there remains one final question: Did Jesus ever claim specific authority to pronounce someone's sins forgiven? We have noticed that the Gospels record two instances in which this appears to be so. Are we on solid historical ground here? Richard Mead has made this a subject of considerable research and has concluded that:

1. The Gospel material on forgiveness is central to the overall tradition. Neither early nor late, the forgiveness

sections appear to be "normal, integral, fully accredited parts of the central stream of synoptic tradition."[32]

2. The Gospel material on forgiveness is congruent with the views expressed in Judaism on this subject.

3. We cannot *prove* that the passage attributing to Jesus the explicit word of forgiveness go back to Jesus,[33] yet the note of an authoritative role in forgiveness had been fully real with Jesus.[34]

4. It is very important to define the relationship between a community that proclaims and offers forgiveness to those who join it, and its faith in the founder of that community. Where did the idea that Jesus forgave sins originate if not in his actual work? Why should it have been introduced if he did not actually exercise this responsibility? Perhaps the paucity of references to forgiveness in the New Testament is actually the strongest evidence that it was such an integral part of the life of the early church that it did not need to be announced. If so, this could come only from the life and teaching of Jesus himself. The proclamation "Your sins are forgiven" finds, then, a quite natural place on the lips of Jesus of Nazareth. It is not nearly all he said, but it was said when it was needed, and by this statement a forgiving community came into existence. Without such a bold statement, it is very difficult to understand how a forgiving community could have arisen to take its place in history and continue for so many centuries.

CHAPTER IX

Paul and the Forgiveness of Sins

G. F. Moore is not the only one to have noticed the strange silence of the great apostle Paul on the doctrine of forgiveness, but he states the problem clearly:

How a Jew of Paul's antecedents could ignore, and by implication deny, the great prophetic doctrine of repentance, which individualised and interiorised, was a cardinal doctrine of Judaism, namely that God, out of love, freely forgives the sincerely penitent sinner and restores him to his favor—that seems from the Jewish point of view inexplicable.[1]

Various ways have been used to get around it. Sanday and Headlam, in their commentary on Romans, concluded that for Paul, justification and forgiveness are the same, and if this is so, then no problem remains.[2] Others have simply ignored the fact that Paul does not use the word, and collected numerous texts that speak more generally of the new life in Christ, thereby leaving the impression that Paul has a good deal to say on the subject.[3]

In the midst of this kind of confusion, it may be helpful to look at the evidence itself. A table of Pauline usage yields the following evidence:

aphiēmi as a verb meaning "to forgive"	Rom. 4:7
aphesis as a noun meaning "forgiveness" (twice):	
aphesis tōn hamartiōn: forgiveness of sins	Col. 1:14
aphesis paraptōmatōn: forgiveness of trespasses	Eph. 1:7
charizomai (as "forgive")with *paraptōmata*	Col. 2:13
charizomai, dative of person and accusative of thing forgiven	II Cor. 2:10c; 12:13 (sarcastically?)
with dative of person alone	Eph. 4:32a,b; Col. 3:13a,b
with accusative of thing alone	II Cor. 2:10b,c
used absolutely	II Cor. 2:7

The term *charizomai*, which clearly stands out as Paul's preference, has taken a new direction through the New Testament understanding of grace. In classical usage the word "grace" (*charis*) meant primarily "graciousness or gracefulness," and the verb *charizomai* meant primarily "to do a favor," both in classical Greek and in the New Testament (for Paul, see I Cor. 2:12; Phil. 1:29). In Philemon 22, in particular, Paul seems to be saying: "I hope that, through your prayers, I will be granted to you." Did Paul prefer the word *charizomai* (twelve out of a total of fourteen usages) because of its root connection with grace? Did it have a softer ring than *aphiēmi?* Did it stress the personal, as the fact that it occurs so often with people rather than sins seems to indicate?

What is clear is that Paul roots his teaching on forgiveness in that which God has done in Christ, and this would fit into his preference for the word *charizomai*. He writes to the Colossians:

Be forbearing with one another, and forgiving, where any of you has cause for complaint: you must forgive as the Lord forgave you. (Col. 3:13, NEB.)

To the Ephesians he wrote a similar admonition: "Be generous to one another, tender-hearted, forgiving one another as God in Christ forgave you" (Eph. 4:32, NEB). It thus seems that for Paul the major interest in forgiveness was for relations within the church. Of course, the phrase "as the Lord" (*kathōs kai ho kurios*, Col. 3:13) is a hard one to live up to. How is it possible for us to live as forgivingly with our fellowmen as Christ was toward us? Paul does not concern himself a good deal with this problem. He is much more impressed with the possibilities of the new life than with the fact that its full potential is never realized. The word "repentance" and its cognates find little usage (four times) in his epistles. No prayer of confession is ever recorded in his letters, and little awareness of guilt can be detected in his epistles.

The question has been vigorously pursued whether Paul did not take a point of view on this matter totally different from that of Jesus himself. Did Paul know the petition "Forgive us our sins" in the Lord's Prayer and use it?[4] Did he know the penitential prayer? A number of scholars agree that he did not know the penitential prayer type. Harder says: "Paul, as a Christian, did not know the penitential prayer."[5] Paul as Christian, as new man, knows only that God through Christ has granted us forgiveness and life. Paul never urges his readers to pray a penitential prayer, and he never expressed the need to experience forgiveness for himself or for his hearers. Nor does he ever mention forgiveness as one of the gifts of salvation given to man in Christ. He neither thanks God for it nor asks for it. His prayers give us the impression that the forgiveness of sins should not be a matter of concern for the Christian. Forgiveness has taken place at the time of baptism. Perhaps he included it in his concept of grace, but it is still significant that he does not explicitly mention it in his prayers.[6] A penitential prayer would simply not fit into his prayers or into his theology.

Paul does not know the Christian who daily experiences remorse for sin and daily recites a penitential prayer, but only the new man, who daily thanks God for his salvation through Christ.[7]

It would seem that every attempt to read a general emphasis on sin into Paul, or to stress the argument from silence, or to argue from the fact that Paul's immediate successors in Asia Minor knew the confessional prayer can only mislead us.[8] Paul's stress is not on man's sinfulness or on forgiveness. In fairness to him and ourselves, we must not read into him what is not there, nor should we stress too much the evidence he provides. He is one important witness to the Christian faith. As such, his experience of the grace of Christ has apostolic authority for us, but his word is not the only word. Perhaps it is an important word, however, and we might do well to place the emphasis where he did. A man with a robust conscience, who places his faith in Jesus Christ and works with confidence, knowing full well that all that he does is human and partial yet can be blessed of God, is better off than one who is obsessed with his unworthiness and sinfulness. Paul was too busy accomplishing God's purpose to bemoan his sinfulness. Such things he could leave behind and press forward to attain his high calling. Although Paul was in no sense perfect, nor did he assume that Christians are perfect, neither was he in any sense hampered by guilt. On the subject of forgiveness, it would seem that those are right who see that when we move from the Hebrew prophets, John the Baptist, and Jesus to Paul, we find ourselves in an entirely different world of thought.[9]

Krister Stendahl concludes his excellent article on "Sin and Guilt in the New Testament" with the observation:

Apostasy is always a terrible possibility in a world in which the Christian is summoned to fight against sin. Yet in spite of this risk he lives in the joyous confidence of his redemption, not in fearful self-evaluation or self-study. Thus, in the New Testament seen as a whole, joy over the forgiveness of sins is more predominant than the zeal to awaken a deep consciousness of sins. In this the total message of the New Testament has remained true to Jesus.[10]

CHAPTER X

The Church as a Forgiving Community

THE COMMISSION OF THE CHURCH

In view of the interest Luke has earlier displayed in the forgiveness of sins, it comes as no surprise to notice that his form of the Great Commission to the church includes the words "that repentance and forgiveness of sins should be preached in his name to all nations" (Luke 24:47). For Luke, this is a central part of the gospel, related in this verse to the death and resurrection of Jesus Christ. In Acts 5:30 f., Peter is described as also seeing such a relationship:

The God of our fathers raised Jesus, whom you killed by hanging him on a tree. God exalted him at his right hand as Leader and Savior, to give repentance to Israel and forgiveness of sins.

Again the forgiveness of sins is connected with both the death and the resurrection of Christ. The exaltation motif, which did not appear in the Gospel passage, occurs here.

According to Luke, the theme of forgiveness was also prominent in Paul's evangelistic proclamation to the Jews. Having referred to the resurrection of Christ, he goes on:

Let it be known to you therefore, brethren, that through this man forgiveness of sins is proclaimed to you, and by him every one that believes is freed from everything from which you could not be freed by the law of Moses. (Acts 13:38 f.)

It is apparent from this that in Luke's view Paul's mission to the Jews is to proclaim the forgiving work of Jesus Christ. If the report of Paul's speech to Agrippa is reliable, then the commission to provide an opportunity for the Gentiles also to receive forgiveness of sins constituted a part of his original confrontation with Jesus on the Damascus road. For, according to Luke, Paul told Agrippa that the Lord then told him that He was sending him to the Gentiles,

to open their eyes, that they may turn from darkness to light and from the power of Satan to God, that they may receive forgiveness of sins and a place among those who are sanctified in me (Acts 26:18).

It is possible that this note was part of Paul's view of the Christian mission. At least the theme of being delivered from the dominion of darkness and being transferred into the Kingdom of God's beloved Son appears again in Col. 1:13 and is immediately followed with the words: "in whom we have redemption, the forgiveness of sins."

If the note of forgiveness were more dominant in Pauline thought, one could be more certain about the genuineness of these passages in Acts. We have already observed that the technical expression used in these passages in Acts for which Luke shows such a predilection never occurs at all in the undisputed Pauline literature. It does occur in Col. 1:14, but it is well known that many scholars do not accept Colossians as coming from Paul's hand. A similar expression occurs in Eph. 1:7 and Col. 2:13 (*aphesis tōn paraptōmatōn* in the former and *charisame-*

nos ta paraptōmata in the latter). Even if we accept the genuineness of both Colossians and Ephesians, as I am inclined to do, the paucity of references to forgiveness in the larger letters of Paul is certainly striking. Anyone who seeks to make forgiveness the dominant motif in the gospel must come to terms with this evidence. The only other place where the idea even occurs is in a quote from The Psalms (Rom. 4:7). Apparently this was not Paul's favorite way of describing the Christian life, at least not to members of the church. Perhaps it was different when he was preaching to unbelievers.

Nevertheless, it would seem from Col. 2:12–13 that he related the forgiveness of sins to baptism. In view of the extent to which this relationship has appeared already in the preaching of John the Baptist, it should not occasion great surprise to notice such a connection in the early church. There were at least some who believed firmly that at the time of baptism a decisive event took place, and the forgiveness of sins at baptism was certainly a belief that was firmly rooted in Christian experience and practice.

However, in certain circles the observance of the Lord's Supper was also related to forgiveness of sins. We have, for example, in the Matthean account of the institution of the Lord's Supper the words: "Drink of it, all of you; for this is my blood of the covenant, which is poured out for many for the forgiveness of sins" (Matt. 26:28). The presence of the words *eis aphesin hamartiōn* is remarkable, because Matthew has had virtually no interest in this formula. From Luke one might have expected it, but hardly from Matthew.

On the other hand, we must note that Matthew does have an interest in the relation between the old and new covenants. The reference in this passage to the covenant that Christ is instituting may have suggested Jer., ch. 31, to Matthew, and that passage explicitly promises, "I will forgive their iniquity, and I will remember their sin no more" (Jer. 31:34). In line with this is Matthew's reluctance to speak of forgiveness of sins in connection with the ministry of John the Baptist, as both Luke and Mark have done. For Matthew, forgiveness of sins must be directly related to the work of Christ and is related to the death of Christ, which is vividly brought to remembrance each time Christians participate in the Lord's Supper.

The Apostles' Creed placed the forgiveness of sins in close connection with the affirmation of faith in the church. This indicates that for the early church forgiveness of sins was not an individual matter, which a person attained in isolated meditation or wrestling with God. Although God is the ultimate source of our forgiveness, and although Christ is the primary agent who achieved forgiveness for man, it is still the church, the empirical church living in history, that serves as God's main instrument in mediating forgiveness. It happens in that proclamation of the church which never allows the emphasis to fall upon guilt-inducing factors but makes dramatically clear that God is forgiving; it happens most vividly in the baptismal experience, when the old passes and the new comes into being and new persons are incorporated into the body of Christ; and it happens weekly as the fellowship gathers around the Table of the Lord and drinks the blood of Christ which has been shed for the remission of our sins.

There is some indication that the declaration, "Your sins are forgiven" was a fixed part of the early kerygma. With reference to I John 2:12–14, Bent Noack says: "If ever in the New Testament, it is in this passage that we can trace the oral preaching; it is only covered by a very thin layer of oral transmission."[1] In C. H. Dodd's well-known study of the apostolic preaching he also concluded that the kerygma always concluded with the offer of forgiveness.[2]

THE AUTHORITY OF THE CHURCH TO
FORGIVE AND RETAIN SINS

Two passages in Matthew's Gospel (chs. 16:18–19; 18:15–22) indicate that Jesus conferred "the authority of the keys" on Peter and the other disciples. John 20:22–23, which describes the giving of the Holy Spirit to the disciples, seems to represent the same idea: "Receive the Holy Spirit. If you forgive the sins of any, they are forgiven; if you retain the sins of any, they are retained." A somewhat similar passage occurs in Luke, ch. 17, although the focus there appears to be on personal rebuke rather than corporate forgiveness.

What are we to make of these passages? One of the simplest ways to dispose of them is to argue that Jesus could not have envisaged a church as coming into existence and that, therefore, these passages go back not to Jesus himself but to the church, which is seeking support for its practice of conferring forgiveness upon its members. Against this it deserves to be said that Jesus obviously intended a new people of God to come into existence rather early in his ministry, after it became clear that as a whole the Jewish people would not accept his message. Certainly the church concept or whether he intentionally founded a group does not depend upon his use of the word "church" or its Aramaic equivalent. As soon as it is granted that he visualized his disciples as forming some kind of group (something that really seems quite evident from the material in the Gospels), any radical rejection of these passages falls by the wayside. Humans generally are so timid about forgiving others, and we have reason to believe that Jews of the first century were even more so, that we are hard pressed to account for these passages in the Gospels if Jesus did not in fact give the church some kind of specific authorization to declare people forgiven.

Those Christians who have often shied away from making such "extravagant claims" as presuming to forgive others have at times shown themselves most adept at using the power of the keys to exclude sinners or to retain sins. Every human society by definition exercises these prerogatives. According to Matthew, the authority to bind and loose is conferred on men (like Peter) who confess who Christ really is. For those who do not believe that Jesus is the Christ, the Son of the Living God, it makes no sense to talk about binding and loosing. This authority is also conferred upon the believers who have followed the steps outlined in Matt. 18:15 f. The power of the kind of community life in which each bears responsibility for the sins of the other, and where an openness prevails that permits us to discuss these with each other, can buy many back from the bondage of sin. Yet its binding and loosing activity is always done with the awareness that Jesus Christ is in their midst (v. 20), that their authority has been conferred upon them through the Holy Spirit, and that without prayer all that they do is vain. However, when all of this accompanies their activity and directs it, they can be assured that what they do on earth is being confirmed in heaven.

Forgiveness thus is seen not as something God alone declares but as a process that he carries out through his community on earth and that finds its ultimate ratification in heaven. If the Jews were scandalized that Jesus of Nazareth would say to a man, "Your sins are forgiven," and accuse him of blasphemy, how much more would they be scandalized to hear that a group of people exercised the privilege of forgiving people their sins? It is a moving tribute to the power of the early church that they did not shrink from this great responsibility and an indication of our weakness that we have so often returned to the notion that only God can forgive sins.

Unfortunately, we have few descriptions of the way this process of communal forgiveness actually worked in the church. Perhaps we know so little about it because it was such a normal part of their experience. There is some indication in the Corinthian correspondence of some difficulties in this area. In I Cor., ch. 5, Paul is distressed about the way in which the incestuous party is being received in the church. He himself has pronounced judgment on the man in the authority given to him by Jesus ("in the name of the Lord Jesus," v. 4). He goes on:

When you are assembled, and my spirit is present, with the power of our Lord Jesus, you are to deliver this man to Satan for the destruction of the flesh, that his spirit may be saved in the day of the Lord Jesus. (Vs. 4–5.)

We observe that the apostolic authority is present, but more important, the Lord himself is present, and what is being done is done by his power. The ultimate goal is the salvation of this man's soul, but in the meantime some drastic measures have to be taken to awaken him to the seriousness of his situation. We do not know what happened to this man and therefore cannot use this as an example of how the church operates as a forgiving community, except that the concern for the person seems to be as important here as the concern for the purity of the church.

In II Corinthians, however, we receive some interesting glimpses into another situation. Having defined his task as not to lord it over them but to work together toward their joy (ch. 1:24), Paul talks about the way in which his previous visit caused them pain, and he does not wish this to happen again, since, "If I cause pain to you, who is left to cheer me up, except he, whom I have offended?" (ch. 2:1, NEB, although I have changed "you" to "he" for *ho lupoumenos*). His writing, he said, came out of much anguish of heart and with many tears. He meant to show them his love through the letter.

Yet he wants it clearly understood that the pain that has been caused has not been to him personally, but "to some extent it has been done to you all." Then follows the passage which is of immediate interest to us:

The penalty on which the general meeting has agreed has met the offense well enough. Something very different is called for now: you must forgive the offender and put heart into him; the man's sorrow must not be made so severe as to overwhelm him. I urge you therefore to assure him of your love for him by a formal act. I wrote, I may say, to see how you stood the test, whether you fully accepted my authority. But anyone who has your forgiveness has mine too; and when I speak of forgiving (so far as there is anything for me to forgive), I mean that as the representative of Christ I have forgiven him for your sake [or that I have forgiven him for your sake, in the presence of Christ]. For Satan must not be allowed to get the better of us; we know his wiles all too well. (Vs. 6–11, NEB.)

If we reconstruct the situation accurately, a disciplinary situation has developed here in which the congregation has been painfully explicit in its condemnation of sin. Paul has undoubtedly contributed to this process in that he has

evaluated the situation, and the binding process has followed the course that seemed to be in harmony with the
will of Christ. There was even a penalty (*epitimia*) agreed
upon by the majority (*hupo tōn pleionōn*), and this is
sufficient (*hikanon*). It is now time for something else, in
fact for the opposite (*tounantion*): to forgive and to put
the heart back into such a one lest he become swamped
by excessive sorrow. The church must change its course
of action. Having, so to speak, taken the heart out of this
person and robbed him of his joy and enthusiasm for life,
they should now replace that heart (the word *parakaleō*
literally means "to encourage"). Since the former course
of action was agreed upon by the majority, so now they
are to assure him of their love "by a formal act" (v. 8).
The verb *kuroō* used here signifies validating something
in a formal way. Does this perhaps mean that the congregation that votes a formal censure must also be prepared
to vote a formal restoration and assurance of love, indeed,
to vote forgiveness?

Verse 10 is difficult to interpret from our perspective.
Literally it should be translated:

But to whom you have forgiven anything, I also, for even that
which I myself have forgiven, if I have forgiven anything [I
have forgiven], on account of you in the presence of Christ
[literally, "before the face of Christ"].

The relationship between apostolic leadership and the
congregation in the forgiving process seems to be at issue
here and also the fact that forgiveness takes place in the
immediate presence of Christ. Paul seems to be saying
the same thing that appears in Matthew's account of the
promise of Christ's presence where two or three are
gathered together for the binding and loosing (Matt.

18:20), or in John, with his promise of the presence of the Spirit in the forgiving and retaining of sins (John 20:22–23). Paul says that when the congregation forgives, it does so in the presence of Christ.

Much discussion has been carried on in contemporary ecclesiology about the nature of the church. We have been told that the church is wherever the Sacraments are correctly administered and where the Word is truly preached. Some would add discipline to this, and still others insist that the church is where Christ is. The Biblical definition of the church provides us with only one mark of the church. Christ is present where people pray for, and assure each other of, the forgiveness of sins. The mark of the authentic church is the ability to realize the forgiveness of sins in the community.

FORGIVENESS AND PRAYER

Not only did Jesus proclaim forgiveness to those who came to him, but he also instructed his disciples to pray for forgiveness (Matt. 6:12; Luke 11:4). The fact that the request for forgiveness found a place within the model prayer in both Luke and Matthew is significant. In addition, both indicate that there is a relationship between our receiving God's forgiveness and others receiving our forgiveness.

According to Matthew, the prayer goes: "And forgive us our debts as also we have forgiven our debtors" (Matt. 6:12). Immediately after the prayer he adds:

For if you forgive men their trespasses, your heavenly Father also will forgive you; but if you do not forgive men their trespasses, neither will your Father forgive your trespasses. (Vs. 14–15.)

The Lucan account is much briefer and reads simply: "And forgive us our sins, for we ourselves forgive every one who is indebted to us" (Luke 11:4).

A similar saying is found in Mark 11:25:

And whenever you stand praying, forgive, if you have anything against any one; so that your Father also who is in heaven may forgive you your trespasses.

The presence of a saying like this in all three Synoptic Gospels emphasizes the importance the doctrine of mutual forgiveness had for the early Christians. It also increases considerably the likelihood that Jesus himself taught this doctrine, and pre-Christian Jewish teachings in this direction would make such a position quite plausible. For instance, Sirach 28:2: "Forgive your neighbor the wrong he has done, and then your sins will be pardoned when you pray," may very well have been known to Jesus.[3]

Krister Stendahl has studied the relation between prayer and forgiveness in Matthew particularly and notes that the underscoring of mutual forgiveness comes as something of a surprise in Matthew's Gospel. The Matthean form of the Lord's Prayer stresses the eschatological manifestation of the Kingdom, and the introduction of the ethical incentive here sounds more like Luke than Matthew.[4] Stendahl has dealt also with the suspicions that Mark 11:25 may be a harmonizing gloss, neither rejecting it decisively nor accepting it. One of the possible reasons for seeing the Marcan saying as occurring at a logical place would be if a close relation between "the power of prayer and the condition of forgiveness and forgiveness could be established."[5] The awareness of a relation between forgiveness and prayer can only be found in the earliest strata of the Gospel tradition, and this is of course strong support for the genuineness of vs. 20–25.[6]

It has often been observed that the parable of the lost sheep has a quite different function in Luke from that which it has in Matthew. In the former, it justifies the association of Jesus with sinners, whereas in Matthew it deals with the erring brother. The emphasis in ch. 18 of Matthew is clearly on forgiving—so much so that it might well be said that for the early Christian church the purpose of all discipline was to bring the brother to an awareness of his sin and thus prepare the road for forgiveness (see Ch. XI). For the young believers, this was an especially difficult, sensitive, but indispensable process. Yet Matthew's main concern in this chapter is that his readers will learn to forgive their brothers from the heart (v. 35). In this process, prayer is seen as such a vital force that Stendahl aptly refers to it as "omnipotent" prayer.[7]

For Matthew it is especially important that the church shall be a place where forgiving neighbors exist side by side. No other mark of the church is given by Matthew except the authority to extend forgiveness to the erring brother. The prayer life of the community cannot be effective unless the channels of forgiveness are clear and forgiveness is being experienced by everyone. Therefore, if while at the place of prayer one discovers that someone else has something against him, the initiative for reconciliation belongs with the one praying (ch. 5:23).

Forgiveness thus cannot be merely received and treasured. It must, to remain active, be mediated to others through those who have received it. No better reminder of that could be given us than the prayer: "Forgive us our debts as we forgive those who are under obligation to us." This does not mean that "by forgiving others, you have given forgiveness to yourself."[8] A relationship exists between our forgiveness and God's. But that is better not defined in any temporal or logical way. Divine and human forgiveness belong together, and when either one is missing, the other suffers a grave deficiency.

FORGIVENESS AND THE CONFESSION OF SINS

The public confession of sins is a common cultural phenomenon, widespread among religious cultures of the ancient past as well as the present.[9] It has been demonstrated that its presence among American Indian tribes antedates the coming of the missionaries, and among the Cágaba in Colombia, South America, a native tells us that before the white man came, everyone lived happily and at peace. "Then they came and all the traditions were lost, the four-day dance, the nine-day dance, confession—they all were dropped." Pettazzoni has remarked that the result of the preaching of the gospel in this case would seem to have been "not the introduction of the practice of confessing sins, but its loss."[10]

The meaning of such confession has been well summarized by Pettazzoni:

The declaration in confession of sin is the evocation of that sin. Thanks to the mystical power of the spoken word, the sin is magically recalled when declared. In savage confessions, it is the magic of the spoken word which is in play. As pronouncing the name of a person is magically equivalent to evoking that person, so when declaring a sin one calls it back, so to say, from the past occasion when it was committed, tears it away in a manner from the person in short, *expresses* it in the proper sense of the Latin *exprimere*, to press out, to extract by pressure.[11]

The key note in confession is deliverance. Confession delivers from the anguish that overcomes a man when tragedy strikes him, and it provides him with an occasion for self-accusation. Because it ministers to this universal human need, its practice is assured among men.

In the religions of the Near East, confession played an important part. Although it would seem that "the Greek world in the classical sense of the word, never knew the confession of sins,"[12] Christianity followed Judaism in giving the confession of sins a place in its practice and theology. It is not found in Roman religion except in the Oriental cults that were brought to Rome, and the fact that confession was fostered by these cults may in fact help to explain their popularity.[13]

Just how important was it in Christianity? The expression "confess your sins" occurs once in the account relating to John the Baptist (Matt. 3:6; Mark 1:5), and apparently describes a part of the conversion experience of the people described in Acts 19:18 who "began confessing and announcing their deeds." Perhaps this occurrence of the verb most clearly signifies the nuance of public declaration, and although from a Christian standpoint it must be assumed that they were confessing *sins,* this is not stated in the text. There remain, however, two texts in which the confession of sins is explicitly recommended by Christian writers.

I John 1:9

The word that is used here for "confess" is not *exomologeō,* which is generally used with "confession of sin," but *homologeō.* It is doubtful that there is any significant difference between these two. Nevertheless, it appears from these few occurrences that *homologeō* is used for sins and the Lordship of Christ, while *exomologeō* is increasingly used for sins alone. The evidence in the apostolic fathers supports our impression. Of seven occurrences in the apostolic fathers, the three occurrences in the Shepherd of Hermas (*vis.* I.i.3; III.i.5; *sim.* IX. xxiii.4) have the formula "confess the sins" (*hamartia*). In the Pseudo-Clementine literature, of the two occurrences, the first uses the verb "confess" with *paraptōmata* (I Clement 51:3), while the second almost gives the impression of the existence of a "confessional," for the writer says that after we have departed from this "world we can no longer make confession" (literally the Greek says: "We are not able to confess or repent there," II Clement 8:3). A similar reference, I Clement 52:1,2, reads: "The Master, brethren, is in need of nothing: he asks nothing of anyone, save that confession be made to him." There would seem to have been a strong development in the direction of public confession of sins according to these texts, but our concern must be first with the text in I John.

In the wider context of John's assertion we note that he confronts his readers with five options (I John 1:6–10). In Greek these are highlighted by the fivefold repetition of an *ean* clause with the subjunctive mood following. These options may be summarized as follows:

If we say we have fellowship but walk in darkness, we lie (v. 6).

If we walk in the light, we have fellowship and cleansing (v. 7).

If we say we are not having sin, we are deceiving ourselves (v. 8).

If we confess our sins, we have forgiveness and cleansing (v. 9).

If we say that we have never sinned, we make him a liar (v. 10).

Obviously, the five options are really only two. One is to face reality, the other is to avoid it and evade it by assuming to be something we are not or by denying conditions as they exist. The second and fourth conditions are positive, because they presuppose that we admit our sins and openly confess them and thus receive forgiveness and cleansing. Is John speaking here of confession in the public or private sense? Or is he assuming that we merely admit to ourselves and to God that we are sinners?

We may well seek to avoid two dangers in interpreting this verse. The one is to see here a fully developed penitential system such as came into existence in the later church.[14] The other extreme is to see here merely an "acknowledgement" of sin (so Brooke) or an inner confession before God.[15] To take the first position is to be a poor historian and to take the second is to be a poor student of language. The word *homologeō* simply never appears to describe a mental process but always an activity that takes place in public. One believes in his heart to be sure, but confesses concretely with his lips (Rom. 10:9).

One must further observe that the word "sin," which heretofore has remained in the singular, now changes to the plural. This would suggest that we confess not sin or sinfulness but specific and concrete sins. The nineteenth-century commentator Erich Haupt has already remarked:

Against sin I cannot contend, and the consciousness of sinfulness in general will not conduce to an effectual repentance; I control sin only by fixing my eye keenly upon its particular outbursts and war against individual transgressions.[16]

We have seen in both our study of the Old Testament (Prov. 28:13) and Judaism that such a practice of confession of sins would not be new. Why, however, this specific interest in it? Were there Gnostics who denied that they were still sinning or that they still belonged among

the sinners? If, as is most often assumed, John is writing to
Asia Minor, then we know that he is writing to people who
are well aware of public confessions in their Oriental religions. Seen from John's view of *koinōnia*, however, it is
clear that sin is committed against both God and man,
and fellowship must be with the Father and with each
other (I John 1:3).

The Jewish idea that through confession release is
granted may very well form the background of the author's
admonition. He certainly does not assume that confession
is a work that we carry out in order to deserve forgiveness.
For Judaism two things were necessary for forgiveness.
There must first be contrite and remorseful confession of
sins, and secondly, absolution of sins. Paul Billerbeck provides a striking example of the way in which the relationship between confession and forgiveness is viewed by one
rabbi.

It is similar to a robber who is being tried before an investi-
gating judge. As long as he raises objections he is punished,
but as soon as he confesses he receives his punishment. God is
different. As long as man does not confess his sins he continues
to receive his condemnation, but as soon as he confesses them,
he is acquitted.[17]

It was recognized that to confess one's sins involved a
certain amount of shame and embarrassment, but better,
they said, experience that here on earth so that we will not
be shamed by God in the next world.[18] The close connection between forgiveness and confession is also seen in the
Book of Jubilees 1:22 where the words "They will not be
obedient till they confess their own sin and the sin of
their fathers" are attributed to the Lord. Baruch 1:14
seems to relate the practice of confession to feast days and

meetings in the house of the Lord. Sirach 4:26 urges the reader: "Do not be ashamed to confess your sins." The most striking parallel to our passage is one in the Psalms of Solomon where the forgiveness of God is also seen as cleansing, is related to confession, and is grounded in the justice of God.

> Unto whom art Thou good, O God, except to them
> 　　that call upon the Lord?
> He cleanseth from sins a soul when it maketh
> 　　confession, when it maketh acknowledgment;
> For shame is upon us and upon our faces on account
> 　　of all these things
> And to whom doth he forgive sins, except to them
> 　　that have sinned?
>
> 　　　　　　　　　　　　　　　(Ch. 9:11 f.)

We can only conclude that the confession of sins spoken of in the New Testament cannot have been anything new for the readers.

John moves on, however, to ground the forgiveness of God in a surprising attribute. We might expect him to say, "For he is merciful and kind to forgive," but instead he says, "If we confess our sins, he is faithful and just to forgive us our sins." Already in the Old Testament we observed that forgiveness is not granted at the expense of God's nature. For the Biblical writers, the forgiveness of God is a function of his righteousness:

Far from forgiveness being a kind of breach of his self-consistency, it is both possible and actual only because God is completely "faithful," completely to be relied upon in all circumstances.[19]

Forgiveness does not violate justice. It is, rather, the highest form of justice that can be done. It not merely restrains the evil and confines it but does so by removing it entirely and changing the person radically, beginning with the central core of his being and moving to his every action. Here, then, is the rock on which our belief in forgiveness is built:

We believe in the forgiveness of sins, not by convincing ourselves that our sins were excusable, or that "we won't do it again." It is because the principle of forgiveness is built into the structure of a moral order created and determined by the character of a just and faithful God.[20]

A confession based on the faithfulness of God brings both forgiveness and cleansing. The word "forgiveness" stresses the forensic aspect; the cleansing stresses the cultic sphere. Sin is a violation of trust in which we incur guilt against God; it is also a stain that pollutes our whole being and leaves its poison in our system. Both cleansing of the stain and cancellation of the obligation are achieved. We are cleansed from the unrighteousness by a righteous God. We lay our lives open to him and need no longer live in a make-believe world, but accept responsibility for our deeds and receive cleansing and forgiveness.

The writer obviously does not visualize forgiveness as a magical ritual, nor does he conceive it as being purely juridical. It is, rather, a personal act taken by a just and faithful God—one who is just in his dealings with men and faithful to his promises.

Yet it is doubtful that the writer conceives of the church as standing idly by while all this happens. Had not the incarnation taught him that God acts in history through human beings? In the Didache, a book written perhaps some forty years after I John, confession of sins took place every week on the Lord's Day just prior to the Eucharist (Didache 12:1). Perhaps when I John was written, the practice of confession had not yet been formalized, but is it farfetched to assume that channels were always available to these churches in Asia Minor by which people oppressed with burdens of sin could find release among their fellow Christians?[21]

CONFESSION OF SINS AND HEALTH

The only clear statement advocating *public* confession of sins in the New Testament is James 5:16. The context in which it appears is worthy of some consideration, since certain elements that we have found elsewhere in the New Testament are brought together here. Although there appear to be a number of separate statements here that have the appearance of being somewhat disjunctive, the literary structure of the rest of the book and of Wisdom Literature in general makes us cautious to assume that various unconnected statements are here thrown together. We suspect that the original writer (or editor) saw a close connection between these various statements, and we will interpret him correctly only if we honor that connection.

He begins this section with two questions: Is anyone feeling badly? Let him pray. Is anyone feeling in high spirits? Let him sing psalms (v. 13).

He then goes on to discuss a more serious sickness and what to do in such a case. If anyone is really sick among them:

1. The sick person should call the elders (v. 14).
2. The elders will (a) pray over him, (b) anoint him with oil in the name of the Lord (v. 14).
3. Their prayer of faith will save (*sōzō*) the sick man (v. 15).
4. The Lord will raise him up and forgive the sins, which he may have committed (v. 15).

After this description of action to be taken in the case of a sick person, he continues: "Therefore confess your sins to one another and pray in behalf of one another so that you may be healed" (v. 16). There is a good deal of power to accomplish things in the prayer of a righteous man (v. 16b). After the illustration of Elijah (vs. 17–18), the writer returns to the theme of sin and prayer and mutual rebuke, but the theme of confession is not directly taken up (vs. 19–20). Perhaps the phrase "saves his soul from death" (v. 20) indicates that the author has not really changed subjects, however.

This intimate union of sin and sickness, forgiveness and health, has cropped up in the Old Testament literature, in the healing of the paralytic, and now comes to prominence here in James.[22] We must begin by rejecting two extremes. James does not say that we are to wait until we are at death's door and then call for the elders. He does not even say that we are to wait until we have exhausted all other means and the sickness seems to be incurable. For him, it is quite natural to call in the resources of the Christian community and to pray. What could be more normal than to avail oneself of the power of prayer and of the support of the community at a time of sickness?[23]

If the passage does not speak about "extreme unction," it clearly does not rule out all medical assistance as thoughtful Roman exegetes have always known and as they are now publicly stating. He does not tell us to call the elders *instead* of the physicians; in fact, it would seem that he is assuming that the elders will use the most widely known medicine of the time, namely, oil! There are those who assume that the oil is seen here as a religious rather than physical element, but such a dichotomy exists only in our minds. It is doubtful that any Biblical writer ever subscribed to such a cleavage. Was the mud Jesus used to heal the blind man a healing agent or a sacramental agent?

Those who object to interpreting oil as a natural healing agent here do so primarily because of the addition of the phrase "in the name of the Lord." But such an objection, although it may accuse those who take it naturally as being influenced by a "modernizing view of medicine,"[24] fails on its side to take the wholeness of the early Christian healing act seriously. To ask whether the oil is to be seen apotropaically, sacramentally, or figuratively is to miss the point. James ascribes the power of healing to the prayer of faith (which apparently he does not restrict to the elders), but he urges the usage of all available resources.

The prayer that is said and the anointment that is given is done under the authorization of Jesus Christ who had also sent the disciples to heal (Mark 6:13). Clearly, what is under discussion here is a miracle cure, but it would seem equally clear that James does not visualize this miracle of healing as taking place outside the context of the fellowship of prayer and visitation and confession that is the church. The elders represent this church not because they have the charismatic gift of healing, although they may also have that, but mainly because they have that maturity which comes as part of eldership. Whether the oil works as a therapeutic agent is a question no more relevant for James than it is for many modern medical men who subscribe to the theory of the French doctor, "I bind his wounds, God heals him." This assumes that behind the act of healing there lie forces that we have not yet been able entirely to encapsulate or to define.[25]

What our author assumes is that there is a relationship between the regular confession of sins to one another and health, and taken in this broad way, no one has ever proved him wrong. The words in James 5:15, "and if he has committed any sins," lead us to think of the natural connection that exists between forgiveness and health. On occasion Jesus also assumed this connection. The passive voice, "they will be forgiven him," may be a Semitic way of saying, "God will forgive him."

After the further statement: "Confess *therefore* your sins to one another and pray for one another," we would expect to read in the second clause: "And thus you will be forgiven," but actually he says "so that ye may be healed." In both instances we must assume that the healing is literal. But why this general admonition to continue mutual confession of sins? Here again the meaning is to be taken broadly. No indication is given to find a trusted brother and confess, nor certainly any suggestion that only the ordained clergy are to receive the confession of their people regularly. The church membership gathered together at each location is to provide for regular public confession of sins.

Paul Althaus has traced in detail the ways in which, from the time of Augustine onward, men began to restrict the meaning of this verse to private confession.[26] From the history of exegesis of this verse it is apparent that private confession cannot be justified from this verse except through exegetical distortion. Its clear meaning is that a Christian congregation can have not only the maturity but also the grace to hear and make a confession, and to extend forgiveness to one another. When such a congregation exists, the church has become both a part of history and of the history of divine salvation.

The sins that are confessed here are not the occasions on which extrasensitive people have been offended by our actions. They are, rather, those occasions when we have raised ourselves against the Lordship of Christ and acted against the sovereign will of God. We are to confess

the sin voluntarily embraced by a self-centered and proud creature, greedy for independence. [Repentance] is sincere contrition aroused by recognition of one's lack of love for God and men. It is essentially the painful realization of a rupture of communion with Jesus Christ.[27]

These words of James and I John which presuppose some means of confession of sin may have more to say to contemporary Protestantism than we imagine at first glance. The deep human need to confess is related to the way in which God has designed that we are to receive forgiveness. Forgiveness is at no place described as the reward we receive for having the courage to confess our sins. Yet in the dynamics of Christian experience it may very well be that the normal way that we experience forgiveness is through the community of forgiveness in which we can confess our sins without fear, knowing that forgiveness is assured, and often health too can come from such an experience.

THE LIMITS OF CHRISTIAN FORGIVENESS

One of the disturbing subjects that comes up most often with people who have sensitive consciences is the question of the unforgivable sin. Especially in mental hospitals one often encounters people who have, according to their own estimation, committed the unpardonable sin. Such people are perhaps looking for an excuse not to accept the forgiveness of God, but it is too simple for us to dismiss them with such a judgment, for too often they are the victims of faulty teaching in the church.

The basis for belief in an unforgivable sin is a difficult saying of Jesus recorded by Luke, Matthew, and Mark with some significant differences:

In Mark 3:28 ff. it appears as follows:

Verily I say to you, that every thing will be forgiven to the sons of men, the sins and the blasphemies whichever they may blaspheme, except whoever blasphemes against the Holy Spirit is not having forgiveness unto eternity but is guilty of an everlasting sin. Because they were saying, He has an unclean spirit.

The context of this statement in Mark is the varying reactions to Jesus' ministry. His friends thought he was mad (v. 21), whereas the scribes who came down from Jerusalem attributed his work to the prince of the devils (v. 22). Even his mother and brothers and sisters had questions about him (vs. 31 f.). Mark says explicitly that Jesus made the statement about the unforgivable sin because they were saying that he had an unclean spirit. According to Mark, then, we could conclude that the sin of blasphemy against the Holy Spirit either is being committed or is in danger of being committed whenever we attribute demonic forces to the power that performs good. Or is this merely a warning that should a person ever blaspheme the Holy Spirit, he will commit a deed so grievous that no forgiveness will be available? The mood of the verb argues for the possibility that Mark does not indicate that someone is actually already blaspheming the Holy Spirit. He merely warns sharply of the possibility of being in a state of mind that while it endures is unforgivable and may indeed become permanent.

Matt. 9:32–34; 12:22–45; Luke 12:8–9

Matthew agrees with Mark in placing the discussion of the unforgivable sin in the context of the claims and actions of Christ. Who is he and from where does he derive power to act? Matthew differs in that he places a specific act of healing at the beginning of the discussion. His precise wording also differs somewhat:

Therefore I tell you, every sin and blasphemy will be forgiven men, but the blasphemy against the Spirit will not be forgiven. And whoever says a word against the Son of man will be forgiven; but whoever speaks against the Holy Spirit will not be forgiven, either in this age or in the age to come. (Ch. 12:31–32.)

Both Luke and Matthew add something not found in Mark, namely, that blasphemy against the Son of Man will be forgiven. They seem thus to differentiate between sinning against the person of Christ and the Holy Spirit. Is it possible that they are also saying that blasphemy against the living Jesus of Nazareth is understandable and forgivable, but once the Holy Spirit has been given, it will be different?[28] It would seem that for Matthew and Luke the saying is addressed primarily to the Jewish opponents of Jesus, whereas for Mark the statement has more general validity and could apply even to his disciples. G. B. Caird writes that blasphemy against the Spirit cannot be forgiven, because to sin against the Spirit is to treat as false that which one knows to be true.

This is the unpardonable sin, not because God is ever unwilling to pardon a penitent, but because an inner dishonesty makes a man incapable of that honest appraisal of himself which is repentance.[29]

Apart from the use the Gospel writers sought to make of this statement, we must ask whether there is any Biblical support for the teaching that men can move beyond the limits of forgiveness. If this possibility exists, when does it come into being and what can be done to avoid it? In asking this question we are certainly not asking an academic question. Many people are seriously distressed and severely depressed because they sincerely believe that they are beyond the limits of forgiveness.

First of all, it would seem clear that all three texts agree in stating that there are limits to forgiveness. Furthermore, all three texts agree in stating that this limit is passed through speaking against or blaspheming the Holy Spirit. Blasphemy means to heap such abuse upon someone that we can imagine nothing good about it at all. It is grievous slander and derision. Notably, our text says that even such blasphemy, if directed against the Son, will be forgiven.

When such blasphemy is directed against the Spirit, it would seem that a more serious degeneration of the person has taken place. Now it is not the Son who stands outside of us who is blasphemed and slandered, but that agent which has been designed especially to relate us to God and dwell in us. In rejecting the Spirit in such a derisive way we are putting ourselves against God's most gracious gift to man, the Spirit. The rejection of this Spirit involves more than merely uttering a formula in which the Spirit is slandered.

"It denotes the conscious and wicked rejection of the saving power and grace of God towards man. Only the man who sets himself against forgiveness is excluded from it."[30]

The Spirit is the strongest token of God's dwelling among men. The murmuring is not against an absent God but against the God who is present among men in the creative and restoring power seen especially in the healing works of Jesus. Schlatter remarks that "the closer God comes to man the more urgent is the duty that man recog-

nize him, and the greater is his guilt when he reviles."[31]
The highest encounter that man has with God is not in
the earthly Jesus but in the coming of the Holy Spirit,
when the actions and attitude of God are made visible
through Him.

The fact that all three writers agree in stating that this
unforgivable sin takes place through the act of speaking
must be taken seriously. Especially, Matthew recognizes
this when he adds the sayings about the way in which the
mouth reveals one's innermost being. Biblical writers do
not think of something as "mere words." Words are powerful carriers of the essence of personality, and they convey
to others what is in the heart. The question that such
words evoke is:

What has happened to this person that he is so hard in his
opposition to the Holy Spirit that he reviles and blasphemes
Him?

Of course it also sharpens our conception of both sin and
forgiveness. Neither is viewed as a magical process that
takes place without the consent of our wills. We are not
mere victims of sin, nor is forgiveness ever thrust upon us.
We are free to reject it. Our text warns us, however, that
it is one thing to ignore it and another to put it aside because of contempt for God's gracious agent of redemption.
To attribute to the devil what belongs to God indicates a
profound unwillingness to choose the good in place of the
bad, and when such an attitude is voiced publicly and
persisted in, there is no forgiveness.

Apostasy in The Letter to the Hebrews

Some other New Testament writers have also pointed
to such a danger with unsparing realism. In the book of
Hebrews the primary reference is to the possibility of

apostasy. In Heb., ch. 6, the writer states that it is impossible to restore again to repentance those

> who have once been enlightened
> who have tasted the heavenly gifts
> who have become partakers of the Holy Spirit
> who have tasted the goodness of the Word of God
>   and the powers of the age to come

if they then commit apostasy, since they crucify the Son of God on their own account and hold him up to contempt (vs. 4–6).

An examination of the Greek text of this passage shows that the verb forms indicating their experience with the gospel and also their apostasy are in the aorist. They have shared in the fruits of salvation but have fallen away and are now recrucifying for themselves the Son of God and holding him up for public ridicule. The change to the present tense in the case of the verbs "renew," "crucify," and "hold up for contempt" would seem to indicate that the author is saying that the two processes cannot go on simultaneously: the process of ridicule and the process of renewal. Repentance is impossible when after such great privileges a deliberate step is taken to depart from them, and when such a step is fortified by continuing ridicule.[32] The limits of forgiveness and renewal are defined by our willingness to receive forgiveness.

The whole argument of Hebrews turns around the conviction that in Jesus Christ something matchless has happened to mankind. Whereas the old system had the disadvantage of reminding people of sin annually, the new system has dealt once and for all with sin, and Christ now awaits the time when all of his enemies will be put under his feet (ch. 10:13). Now that forgiveness of sins has come, there is no longer any offering for sins (v. 18). This forms the basis of his appeal to his readers. He especially points out that those who violated Moses' law died without mercy (v. 28).

How much worse punishment do you think will be deserved by the man who has spurned the Son of God, and profaned the blood of the covenant by which he was sanctified, and outraged the Spirit of grace? (V. 29.)

The three things he has done show his utter contempt for the acts of mercy and love God has shown us in Jesus Christ. The author argues that greater love shown to us, if rejected, incurs greater guilt. He does not read from the mercy of God that God is tolerant and allows us to mock his mercies. He concludes that portion of his argument with the words: "It is a fearful thing to fall into the hands of the living God" (v. 31). Did he not know that David (II Sam. 24:14), when given the choice, preferred to fall into the hands of God rather than man, knowing that God's judgment is much to be preferred to that of men? The writer of the book of Sirach also expressed this point of view when he said: "Let us fall into the hands of the Lord, but not into the hands of men; for as his majesty is, so also is his mercy" (ch. 2:18). It is reported that John Donne said: "If it is a fearful thing to fall into the hands of God, it is an even more fearful thing to fall out of his hands."

The writer of Hebrews is aware of the gravity of his message both here in ch. 10 and in ch. 6. In both places, after these difficult words he proceeds to remind them of the integrity and strength of their faith as it has been demonstrated in the past. This should counteract the fear of those who need such reassurance.

The illustration of Esau used in ch. 12:16 serves, however, to tell us that human experience sometimes cannot be undone. There are moments in life that never return; there are opportunities that if squandered are lost forever. Herein lies the warning of the writer to the Hebrews. It would be cruel to suggest to people that there will always be a chance to undo their past. Certain events, perhaps all events, are really unique because they will never occur under exactly the same conditions again. The person who betrays Christ, who reviles the work of God, may become so changed in his life and attitude that the desire to be forgiven may never arise. What then remains but to await the judgment of God?

THE SIN UNTO DEATH IN I JOHN

The First Letter of John also seems to touch on this question in the enigmatic reference to the "sin unto death" (ch. 5:16–17).

If any one sees his brother committing what is not a mortal sin, he will ask, and God will give him life for those whose sin is not mortal. There is sin which is mortal; I do not say that one is to pray for that. All wrongdoing is sin, but there is sin which is not mortal.

On the one hand, we may find it surprising that this author would refer to a sin that is not mortal. Do not all sins lead unto death (Greek, *eis ton thanaton*)? The expression seems to mean an act that deserves the death penalty (Testaments of the Twelve Patriarchs, Issachar, ch. 7; Jubilees, chs. 13; 33; cf. also, Num. 18:22 and Isa. 22:14). It has become common to relate this "sin unto death" to blasphemy against the Holy Spirit of the Gospels or to the apostasy referred to in Hebrews.

Reinhold Seeberg has proposed a different solution to the problem.[33] He reasons that John cannot be speaking of an unforgivable sin, since he says in I John 1:7,9, that the blood of Christ cleanses us from *all* sin and that God forgives us every unrighteousness. Furthermore, in ch. 5 not a word is said about the sin being unforgivable. Matthew 12:31 has as its core the word of impossibility to forgive, and Heb., ch. 6, the impossibility of renewal. In I John we must therefore rule out any idea that the sin is unforgivable. What is being discussed is the advisability of intercession in behalf of this sinner. Seeberg points out that the energetic denunciation of the incestuous man in I Cor., ch. 5, does not rule out his forgiveness but in fact has this as its purpose. Even the fact that in the Old Testament intercession is withheld (Jer. 7:16; 11:14; 14:11 f.) on occasion, and that sometimes a sin is unforgivable (I Sam. 3:14; Isa. 22:14), should not mislead us here. It is, moreover, apparent that John is not thinking of a specific sin, since he used the word without the article and thus would seem to be thinking of a class of sins. The reference cannot be to heresy but must be to some action that is discernible with the eye. Seeberg sees in the "sin unto death" the serious sins described in the documents of the Two Ways (Didache, chs. 1–6). Accordingly, John would have in mind the serious pagan sins that are found in the various lists of vices in the New Testament. He may have in mind such sins as sexual incontinence, greed for possessions, or pride (I John 2:16).

Why should people who are victims of these sins be denied intercession? Seeberg feels that the people referred to are Christians who have retained the ordinary sins of the pagans and unabashedly carry them on in their daily lives. The total congregation must act on these matters, and personal intercession should not precede the action of the group. John is concerned that everyone participate in the general confession. Forgiveness is possible, but it must

be made available through the action of the whole congregation as the guilty one confesses. The older practice
of Matt. 18:15 may be contrasted here, for it seems to
open the door to intercession for the serious sinner as well.
For John this appears to be dangerous. Nothing can be attained with such serious sinners without their own participation and that of the congregation. Through your intercession, they might seek to avoid confession before the
whole congregation, and this John does not visualize as
advantageous.[34]

It would seem that some interpretation such as that of
Seeberg's best fits the picture here as well as that presented in the whole New Testament. It is the sin of the
brother that is under discussion and not that of the enemy,
for both Jesus and Stephen prayed for the enemy.

We have before us, then, an example of the intimate
relation that exists between intercession and prayer. There
is great power in intercession, but there is also some pros-
pect that it might be misused. John does not say that his
reader is not supposed to pray for the one committing a
sin unto death. He is simply withholding his admonition
to pray for him. Such reticence is surely not born out of
skepticism that God can restore or forgive the sinner. It
is quite possible, however, that it is born of the conviction
that prayer if practiced alone is of limited value when
deliberate sin of a serious nature is involved. To experience
forgiveness, more is needed than merely the prayer of one
individual on behalf of another. Prayer for forgiveness is
most effectual when it is practiced in the presence of the
factors of personal rebuke and admonition and binding
and loosing that both Matthew and James as well as the
Gospel of John recommend.

We may agree with R. Schnackenburg, who says that "in
the Christian church each believer has, thanks to his rela-

tionship to God made possible by Christ, the intention to rescue the erring brother."[35] Although he considers the conjecture of Seeberg devoid of analogous New Testament texts, he correctly observes that the "sin unto death" is not to be identified with either the sin against the Holy Spirit or the apostasy of the book of Hebrews.

I John 5:16 deals primarily not with the repentance of man but with God's willingness to forgive, which is appealed to in brotherly intercession; the brothers are in a certain sense similar *paraklētoi* on earth as Christ is in heaven (ch. 2:1).[36]

We may be certain that the "unforgivable sin" has not been committed by those who are concerned about it. To such, one could speak another word also recorded by John: "If our heart condemns us, God is greater than our hearts and he knows all things" (I John 3:20). Therefore, we reassure ourselves before him. The greatness of God is no reason to fear, for his awesome greatness is most clearly demonstrated in the infinite love he has shown us in the face of Jesus Christ. It is especially important to him that the bruised reed and the smoldering wick not be broken or quenched (Matt. 12:18–21).

To those afraid that they have committed the unforgivable sin one can say unequivocally that they have not committed it. Perhaps more important than such words would be our willingness to listen to them so that as they confess, we can assure them of the forgiveness of sins, not only through our words but above all through our actions.

Augustine said in describing the unforgivable sin:

This is the hardness of heart even to the end of this life, which leads a man to refuse to accept remission of his sins in the unity of the body of Christ, to which life is given by the Holy Ghost. . . . It cannot be proved to have been committed by any one, till he has passed away from life.[37]

Part Four

FORGIVENESS IN THE LIFE OF THE CONTEMPORARY CHURCH

CHAPTER XI

Forgiveness and the Discipline of Grace

RECOGNIZING THE NEED FOR DISCIPLINE

It is characteristic of Protestantism that almost nothing positive can be said about church discipline. To many the word itself suggests something distasteful and brings up memories of Geneva at its worst or heresy-hunting in the sects. Nevertheless, there is an increasing conviction that unless discipline is restored to a position of respect and vital influence, the Protestant Church may very well be doomed to an insignificant existence or, eventually, to total oblivion.

Evidence for the recognition of the need for discipline is seen in Martin Marty's incisive analysis of the current dilemma of the American church on that rare occasion when he goes beyond analysis to suggest some aspects in which the difference between the church and the world can be made observable. The four areas that he lists include discipline.[1] To be sure, discipline gets the briefest treatment of the aspects Marty mentions, but the fact that it is mentioned at all is worthy of note.

A Scottish theologian come to America, Geddes Mac-
Gregor, has offered a slashing critique of the laxity of
Protestantism and attempted to rally the Reformed tradition around a movement to restore discipline to a strong
and vital place in the church. Beginning with a study of
the Reformation doctrine of the church, MacGregor notes
that for Luther one of the seven marks of the church was
discipline. Discipline was stressed even more by Calvin,
who thought he could learn from Luther that true doctrine
without discipline is not enough. Consequently, Mac-
Gregor concludes,

To Word and Sacrament the Reformed Church added, however, Discipline, not because the union of Word and Sacrament
is not enough in itself, but because without Discipline it becomes a mockery. It may be that it is in the recovery of the
ministry of Discipline, which flows from the mystery of the
divine *agapē* itself, that the Church will more fully express
and so make more visible its wholeness as *corpus Christi*.[2]

MacGregor elaborates this theme to some extent in a
more recent book entitled *The Coming Reformation*. Ob-
serving that the very word "discipline" sounds archaic to
modern Protestant ears, he asserts that it remains absolutely indispensable for the life of the church. Charging
that too often discipline has been driven out by the temptation to cater to those with money, he calls for its revival
alongside of the revival of liturgy and personal mystical
devotion. One of the reasons why many church members
are attracted to clubs and fraternities outside the church
is that they experience a type of discipline there that is
missing in the church. As many laymen can testify, they
are often asked to memorize more Scripture upon joining
a Masonic lodge than before joining the church.

Certainly MacGregor's analysis of the situation is correct at many points. When he notes that many people

would not give up a horseradish for Christ, although they are willing to discipline themselves severely in the interests of a more modest waistline, and that fear of cancer is much more disciplinary in its results than the ranting and thundering of the church about the use of tobacco, he is certainly correct. Whether the positive solution that he offers—moving toward the use of bishops in the Presbyterian Church—is the best one or whether one should place as much emphasis on correctness of doctrine as he does are moot questions.[3] For one thing, it is highly questionable that the denominations which have bishops have been more successful than other churches in maintaining meaningful discipline.

In the Chalmer Lectures, published in 1960 by John Kennedy, the theme of discipline is taken up at considerable length. Kennedy also talks of the irrational prejudice against church discipline and begins with the assumption that at the present time active loyalty to the church is practiced only by a minority of its members, and the majority has no healthy respect for either the authority or the discipline of the church. He calls for a return to the authority of the Bible, a return to a conception of authority in church government, but then makes the correct observation that the main reason for the coolness regarding church discipline is not a purely administrative matter but a falling away from the religious principles that animated the Reformers. In Calvin's view of discipline as "the nerves of religion" we have an important practical aspect of the church's life. Discipline, Kennedy insists, must provide the gaping lack in the congregational life, namely, the member's concern for the integrity of the fellowship of believers. In order to make this possible, small groups, perhaps house churches, should be formed. He quotes Evelyn Underhill with approval:

The vitality of personal Christianity will only be fostered in small groups where the members feel responsible for one another, learn from one another, and awake to creative life again in the experiential knowledge of what the beloved community is in faith and action.[4]

Karl Barth has also dealt with the subject several times. At one point, he discusses the question in the context of church law and concludes:

There is no such a thing as church discipline—possibly it is a misunderstanding and misuse even of the words about the keys of the kingdom (Matt. 16:19) when they have been interpreted as such—in which it is man's prerogative to decide which people are members of Christ's body and hence true Christians, are consequently saints and which are not.[5]

Thus he rejects the idea of church discipline if we mean thereby that one human being can decide whether another belongs to Christ's body. Later, however, he speaks more positively of it as the only means whereby the confession of the church can be kept pure, the requirements of Baptism defined and fulfilled, admission to the Lord's Supper limited and defined, but above all, whereby the confession may not only be expressed but carried out corporately. Barth prefers to speak, however, of the discipline by which the Lord himself directs the life of the congregation. It is the church that is put under discipline and kept in church discipline. He rejects the position of the enthusiasts who leave everything to the Holy Spirit, because precisely when you leave it to the Holy Spirit, it is not left to haphazardness and to any slowpoke routine. Rather, all questions are solved through a common conscientious searching of the Scriptures to determine what constitutes obedience in that particular case.[6]

Perhaps most difficult for a contemporary reader to comprehend is the attention that church discipline receives in Eduard Thurneysen's *A Theology of Pastoral Care*. Here the second chapter deals with church discipline, and the attempt is made to go back to the founders of the Reformed church, Luther, Bucer, and Calvin, for support. Church discipline is seen primarily as a device in the care of souls, namely, admonition. Through church discipline the church guards the power that goes out from Word and Sacrament in such a way that it may become realized. Without such church discipline there is no actual church. Through church discipline the pastoral task is firmly grounded in the total work of the church. The goal of discipline is to win people for the Kingdom of Christ and his church on the earth.[7]

It would be wrong to leave the impression that the concern for church discipline has come primarily from Reformed or Presbyterian writers. One is surprised, for example, to find in Rudolf Bultmann's *Theology of the New Testament* a section on church discipline, the first time such a section has ever been inserted in a theology of the New Testament.[8] Bultmann's concern is not with a description of the New Testament teaching but with its development in the early church.

The concern with church discipline in the present life of the church was expressed particularly by Gerhard Ebeling in 1947. He declared:

As surely as the teaching of justification by faith alone is the article of faith on which the church stands or falls, so surely genuine confession of this teaching actualizes itself in the correct understanding and practice of church discipline.[9]

He concludes his lecture with the statement, "I know of no other problem that oppresses the church so much, and whose solution is more urgent, basic, and far-reaching than the problem of church discipline."[10] In the conviction that Luther's own statements and practice on this matter are of relevance for the present-day church, studies have been devoted to his practice of church discipline.[11]

THE MEANING OF "DISCIPLINE"

If discipline is now looked at again, the reasons behind this deserve mention. First of all, the method used here will be primarily one of Biblical interpretation. The Reformers can be instructive for us, but they cannot bind us. Certainly it is clear that both Luther and Calvin relied heavily upon the authority of the state in all their attempts at church discipline, and their philosophy of church discipline also was greatly determined by their view of church-state relations. Luther clearly stated that church discipline would be superfluous if the state would be thorough enough in its law enforcement.[12]

Thus if we are to get any help from the Reformation on this point, we need to look to the free-church movement, the Anabaptists. Among their brotherhoods it was recognized that a separation had to be made between the role of the constable and that of the church leader. Rejecting as they did the identification of church and state, they had the responsibility of demonstrating that the church could develop procedures of dealing redemptively with the deviants. They saw the function of the church not as restraining the evildoer but of retraining him to do good after the resources of Christ and the church were made available to him. Their attempt to build strong Christian communities was remarkably successful in spite of such widely publicized debacles as transpired at Münster. Even at Münster, however, it is not often recognized that one major factor in the violence there was the forceful breakdown of all meaningful communication between the various elements of the city population. Those who still identify the whole left wing of the Reformation with the revolutionaries make a mistake similar to that of the modern person who identifies the civil rights movement with the Black Muslims and can see riots as the only result of the movement.

That meaningful discipline was practiced and seen as the institutionalization of forgiveness is especially clear in a recently discovered manuscript. It is a confession written by one Helen von Freyberg, a member of the nobility and of the brotherhood that was led by Pilgram Marpeck. From this confession it becomes clear that she is guilty primarily of refusing to accept the counsel of the group. Anyone reading the document with the anticipation of getting juicy details about her sins will be disappointed. Although it was written down because she could not bear to speak it publicly, we are never really told what the precise sin is for which she was being admonished. Yet the document itself indicates that discipline can be a truly redemptive experience and can lead to the forgiveness of sins.[13] Adequate as these ways may have been for the sixteenth century and instructive as they may be, their usefulness for us today still remains open to discussion.

Our study of discipline cannot be exhaustive. A systematic attempt has been made to study all the New Testament passages on discipline, and although that study has its limitations, no attempt is here made to improve upon it.[14] Since most often forgiveness and discipline are not related, to the impoverishment of both, and since they appear to be viewed as parts of one process in the New Testament, we will confine ourselves to those passages of Scripture in which forgiveness of sins and discipline are related.

It is often asserted that the concept of church discipline does not occur as such in the New Testament. A study of the New Testament does not support that claim. The Greek word that comes closest to our English word "discipline" is the word *paideuō*. In its various forms it occurs twenty-one times in the New Testament. Of these twenty-one times, the New English Bible fifteen times translates it with the word "discipline." When one compares this with the King James Version, which used the word "discipline" only once in the whole Bible (Job 36:10), or with the Revised Standard Version, which used the word "discipline" nine times in the New Testament, it is evident that this new version reflects the added interest in discipline found among Biblical scholars today. The question remains, however, whether the translators are faithful to the original in translating it in this way.

Originally the term referred to those who occupied their time primarily with children. From that it came to refer to education and is used in that sense in a number of places in the New Testament (Eph. 6:4; Rom. 2:20; Acts 7:22; 22:3) and has the derived (or perhaps for them, basic) meaning of "flogging" in Luke 23:12,22.

From this more or less secular usage it is applied to the religious life in Heb., ch. 12, which contains nine of these occurrences. It is a chapter that urges the readers to struggle against sin with courage and joy. Here the analogy between the earthly father and the heavenly Father is developed at some length. No indication is given to help us to see the nature of this discipline. Our interpretation of the wider context would lead us to believe that it is the wrestling with sin that is itself the discipline to which the Christian is subjected. In this discipline the readers are to see definite proof that they are sons of God. The purpose of this discipline is for their good, that they may share his holiness (v. 10). Jesus is their example, and, having this example, they are to attempt to strengthen the whole brotherhood (vs. 12–17), taking as a warning the experience of Esau. The lame are to be healed, and it is the responsibility of the brotherhood "that no one fail to obtain the grace of God" (v. 15).

In line with general late Jewish thought, Paul also refers to falling under the Lord's judgment as discipline, which is meant to save us from being condemned with the rest of the world. This comment is made in connection with certain irregularities within the Corinthian church, and perhaps he sees the fact that a number of them are feeble and sick and a number have died as evidence of this disciplining judgment. In any case, it is clear that he sees it as redemptive (I Cor. 11:32). Likewise, he sees the suffering that is the lot of the Christian as a part of the discipline of God (II Cor. 6:9). The same motif uniting discipline and love is seen in Rev. 3:19, where discipline is described as evidence of love.

When we ask about the means that the Lord uses to discipline his own, we find that the Scriptures are given for that purpose. Their aim is to reform manners and to provide discipline in right living so that "the man who belongs to God may be efficient and equipped for good work of every kind" (II Tim. 3:16–17). Reference is here made exclusively to the Old Testament, and it is these Scriptures which are to make us wise and lead to salvation through faith in Jesus Christ (v. 15). Accordingly, Christ being the final word of God, one writer of the New Testament says that the grace of God, which is almost certainly to be seen as an equation for Jesus Christ,

has dawned upon the world with healing for all mankind; and by it we are disciplined to renounce godless ways and worldly desires, and to live a life of temperance, honesty, and godliness in the present age, looking forward to the happy fulfilment of our hopes when the splendour of our great God and Saviour Christ Jesus will appear" (Titus 2:11–13, NEB).

From this passage, it is apparent that discipline is seen as a fruit of the great power that has come to man in Jesus Christ. Thus discipline is meant primarily to rescue the sinner from the enslavement of a way of life that Christ has made obsolete.[15]

It is apparent that the church has a responsibility here to all its members. Mention is made of two men who made shipwreck of their faith and who were then consigned to Satan "in the hope that through this discipline they might learn not to be blasphemous" (I Tim. 1:20, NEB). Once it is made possible for the member of the church or the leader to exercise this discipline, there is the danger that he will not exercise it in the spirit of Christ himself, and, therefore, the admonition is that the ideal teacher is one who is "gentle when discipline is needed for the refractory" (II Tim. 2:25, NEB). That such a warning is needed has been demonstrated repeatedly throughout the history of the church.

It is necessary to look at certain passages in greater detail in an attempt to understand the way in which the early church saw the process of forgiveness related to discipline.

The passages selected will indicate that our working definition of church discipline is: *Church discipline is that*

*process whereby God's community submits to the direc-
tion of its risen Lord, who judges, exhorts, reproves, and
rebukes the presence of sin so that through forgiveness the
whole community may enjoy his presence.* It is assumed
that the Word is the primary instrument in this process,
the Word as written in Scripture and as continually interpreted by the Holy Spirit. The integral part prayer has
in this process has already been noted.

What differentiates this definition from others? Rudolf
Bohren defines church discipline as "rejection of sin and
thereby preserving the holiness within the church."[16] Bultmann also sees it primarily as a means to preserve the
purity of church in both conduct and teaching.[17] Although
our definition agrees for the most part with Thurneysen's
general description of discipline, it includes (against
Thurneysen) the aspect of judgment.[18] With MacGregor
we stress that Christian discipline is not primarily interested in building regulations or rules; "it is for the upbuild-
ing of Christian character and the correction, in charity,
of the faults that impede this." It is the "principal instrument of our sanctification," and to lack it "is to be ignorant
of the very meaning of the Christian life. Discipline is the
yoke of Christ."[19] Discipline seen in this light fully recognizes the dangers of Pharisaism, which Thurneysen justi-
fiably seeks to avoid, and accepts the position that the
perfect church, the community without spot and wrinkle,
is a promise for the future, not something that can ever be
attained on earth.

On the other hand, contrary to much of modern theological thought, the New Testament seems to emphasize
the radical change that has already taken place, thanks
be to Christ, rather than the distance yet to go or the
impossibility of ever attaining perfection. For Christians,
to believe that Christ's main purpose in coming to earth

was to uncover the cesspool of human sin in such a way as to put an end to all Pharisaism, and to consider it a virtue to be enabled to say: "What a bad boy am I!" certainly does less than justice to the incarnation. If neo-orthodoxy has shown us that the liberal portrait of man was wrong, it has yet to reflect the throbbing conviction of the New Testament that profligate Corinth, idolatrous Ephesus, and speculative Colossae could become colonies of heaven. For precisely when it is asserted that pride is the worst sin and that it is evidence of pride to recognize another's sin, the necessity for discipline evaporates. For discipline believes that sin is alien to the body of Christ and that there is a difference between church and world. It is not by accident, therefore, that the younger churches have always had a more vigorous discipline, for in a mission context the lines between church and world tend to stand out more sharply.[20]

In church discipline we are dealing with the progressive eradication of sin. Part of the reason for the demise of church discipline is that its patterns have been applied to the perpetuation of social practices of denominations. People have been excommunicated for habits such as smoking and drinking, to say nothing of certain innovations in the area of dress, with an appeal to Scripture! That the New Testament would have no share in a picayune attempt to construct social barriers is clear on every page, and when contrasted with the Qumran sect, cannot be evaded. For among the Qumranites the machinery of discipline went into action for such offenses as interrupting a speech at one of their discussions (ten days' penitence) and deliberately reclining to sleep during the discussion (a month's penitence) (1QS VII, 9–10). No one was permitted to leave the compound without permission, and anyone who spat in the presence of the "Great Ones" had to do penance for a month (1QS VIII.13). Conspicuous gestures, intemperate laughter, vain speeches, brought ten, thirty, and ninety days of penitence respectively. Even a gesture with the left hand was punished by ten days (1QS VII.13–16).

It should thus be clear that church discipline is not primarily concerned with order in the community life but with the presence of sin. On matters such as eating and drinking foods considered suspect by other believers, rules could not be applied. Freedom to follow one's conscience, love for the brother who is weak, faith in Jesus Christ, but above all, the conviction that the Kingdom of God consists not in food and drink but in righteousness, peace, and joy (Rom. 14:14) determine the church's attitude toward those actions of life not defined as sin.

This whole area of life has been known as adiaphora ever since the sixteenth century, and it has been assumed that the New Testament permits us to speak of adiaphora. This is, however, a Stoic concept and finds no place in the New Testament. It is doubtful that Paul would ever say that there is a no-man's-land in Christian ethics; what he does say is that a given act can be either good or bad depending upon the reaction it receives from the "brother for whom Christ died" (v. 15).

Church discipline is meant to assist the community in making these decisions. As Bavinck says:

In church discipline the community recognizes that the gift of new life given to us in Christ confronts each member with new decisions. Thus it is not surprising that church discipline is earnestly practiced almost everywhere in the younger churches.[21]

The process of church discipline as described in the New Testament went through a number of phases, depending to a large extent on the degree of response received. Its goal was always to prevent sin or to achieve the forgiveness of sins, and thus it is not necessary that all phases be carried out to the end. The various phases deserve closer study.

CHURCH DISCIPLINE AND JUDGMENT

In our justified reaction to moralism we have become extremely hesitant to think of the church as a "judging society." We prefer to talk about acceptance and educate ourselves to become as nonjudgmental as possible in our dealings with people. That this has a degree of validity certainly cannot be questioned. John tells us that God did not send his Son into the world "to judge the world, but that the world through him might be saved" (John 3:17). This same Jesus is never represented in the Gospels as preaching sermons of condemnation to the crowds or trying to awaken a "sense of sin or guilt" among them. One observes especially in his dealings with the Samaritan woman (ch. 4) and the notorious sinners that his knowledge of their sin is conveyed only obliquely if at all.

Yet there is evidence that Jesus did use his critical faculties to weigh the good and the bad and to reprimand the ones who had committed themselves to the bad. What is striking is that these reprimands are always given either to his own disciples (the weak in faith) or to those who claimed that they were the true seed of Abraham. And in such a context Jesus explicitly says, "For judgment I came into this world, that those who do not see may see, and that those who see may become blind" (ch. 9:39).

The disciples likewise are told: "Judge not that you be not judged" (Matt. 7:1), and again they are told that "by their fruits ye shall know them" (vs. 15 f.), and this is the standard they are to use in determining whether a given prophet is false or not. Accordingly, it is clear that the community of God's people must continually weigh and evaluate all the "spirits" that arise in its midst, as well as continually prove the quality of its life. Paul tells the Corinthians that "A man gifted with the Spirit can judge the worth of everything, but is not himself subject to judgement by his fellowmen" (I Cor. 2:15, NEB). Later he affirms that he himself is not the least concerned about their judgment of him, not because he thinks that he is above their evaluation, but because he knows that his case rests with a higher court from which everyone will receive commendation (ch. 4:3,5). Some indeed have a special charismatic gift, the ability to distinguish between spirits (ch. 12:10), but the spirits of the prophets are subject to the prophets (not vice versa), and therefore one can never abdicate responsibility for evaluation by taking refuge in the Spirit (ch. 14:32). For the writer of I John the "testing of the spirits" is an obligation that rests upon each believer in the fellowship (I John 4:1 f.). While certain elementary creedal criteria are given, the essential question is well expressed at the end of Paul's second letter to Corinth:

Examine yourselves, to see whether you are holding to your faith. Test yourselves. Do you not realize that Jesus Christ is in you? Unless indeed you fail to meet the test! (II Cor. 13:5.)

This kind of evaluation takes place through letters written by the apostles, by personal visits, and other means. It takes on a specific form in *exhortation* (*parakaleō*). One of the problems in discussing this aspect is that the word *parakaleō* has, since Wycliffe's and Luther's versions, been translated with the word "comfort" or *trösten.* Although these translations were not too far amiss, given the meaning of "comfort" in their day, they certainly miss it for contemporary usage. It is true that "comfort" is included in the meaning of the Greek word, but it by no means exhausts its meaning.

Sensing this, Norman Snaith has argued that the word "paraclete" means "convictor" rather than comforter. His position is based on the assumption that *parakaleō* is the equivalent in this respect to the Hebrew word *nacham,* which means to "comfort *out of* sorrow," and not "comfort in sorrow." According to Snaith, it involves the cessation of sorrow, since the root is often associated in the Old Testament with the idea of change of mind, heart, and intention. It is thus a conversion word even in the Fourth Gospel.

The Holy Spirit is not that Spirit which comforts the disciples after the Lord Jesus has been glorified, but rather that Spirit which convinces them of the truth of the things of Christ.[22]

Johannes Behm rejects this interpretation as "neither semantically nor exegetically tenable."[23] Although a rejection of this interpretation as exclusive seems justified, we may question whether Behm does not go too far in rejecting it as "exegetically untenable." The work of the *paraklētos* is defined in John 16:8 as "convicting the world concerning sins," etc., and regardless of the way one translates *elenchō* in this verse ("reprove," KJV; "convict," RV; "convince," RSV, NEB; "*strafen!*" Luther), the essential goal of the process seems to be as Snaith suggests: to move the world out of the sorrow of sin into the joy of freedom from it.

The progression of these steps is particularly clear in II Cor., ch. 7, where Paul refers to the comfort with which he is filled and the joy that came as a result of knowing that the grief they had experienced was a godly grief leading them to repentance. It would appear that one of the meanings of *parakaleō* is definitely "to address in the form of an admonition."[24] This meaning predominates in the book of Acts and in the Pauline letters and focuses on the intent to win the hearer to commitment for the apostolic proclamation. Paul gives expression to this when he says:

In behalf of Christ, therefore, we come as his ambassadors. It is as if God were exhorting[25] you through us. We beseech you in behalf of Christ: Get reconciled with God. (Ch. 5:20.)

The exhortation takes place in the context of beseeching, not threat, yet there is a seriousness about it which indicates that something important beyond description is at stake. It has elements of reproof, but also shades of warning; it partakes of what we call advice, but it is stronger than that. It is an appeal (I Thess. 2:3), and the continuous exhortation of the Holy Spirit caused the church to continue to grow (Acts 9:31). Through the power of the Spirit the church confronted others with the call to repentance, offering them the gospel, and the result was a growing church.[26]

The word occurs also in ch. 2:40 in an evangelistic context, and should there be rendered "exhort." Luke already uses it to describe the preaching of John the Baptist (Luke 3:18).

The relationship of judgment to forgiveness is finely put by Søren Kierkegaard:

Commonly the situation is conceived thus: justice means severe judgment; love is the gentle thing which does not judge, or if it does, love's judgment is a gentle judgment. No, no, love's judgment is the severest judgment ever passed upon the world, more severe than the flood, more severe than the confusion of Babel.[27]

Judgment can be the clearest evidence of love, even for the physician.

PERSONAL REBUKE

There appears to be another step in this process that intensifies the element of rebuke somewhat. An example is John the Baptist in Luke 3:19 who had *reproved* (*elenchō*) Herod for having Herodias, his brother's wife. Thus we have moved here from admonition to rebuke, from warning to exposure. A study of the ways in which the term *elenchō* occurs in the New Testament supports this. Before looking at the New Testament usage we may observe that in no sense is this a novel conception of Christianity. The term *elenchō* is widespread in Greek writings, occurring already in Homer in the sense of "shaming" or "exposing to ridicule." According to Friedrich Büchsel, the following meanings developed: (*a*) to shame or embarrass through persuasion or refutation, (*b*) to reprimand, (*c*) to persuade, refute, (*d*) to call attention to, (*e*) to examine or investigate. Although the basic meaning is hard to determine, it would seem to be "to go to the root of an evil matter that is embarrassing or shameful to someone else."[28]

In the Greek Old Testament it is used alongside of *paideuō*, which stresses the fatherly aspect of God's instruction to emphasize the judgmental aspect of God's dealing with men.[29] It is within the context of Judaism that this concept is applied most clearly to human relations. Beginning with Lev. 19:17 f.:

> Thou shalt not hate thy brother in thy heart. Thou shalt not
> fail to reprove thy fellow and not bear sin because of him . . . .
> Thou shalt love thy neighbor as thyself

but going beyond this to a serious evaluation of sin and its
consequences, the importance of reproving one's brother's
sins was often discussed. It was observed that to fulfill
this precept was extremely difficult, especially when the
person who took the initiative was also the aggrieved
party. George Foot Moore tells us that several teachers
testify to the difficulty,

> one declaring that in that generation there was no one able
> thus to reprove his fellow, another there was no one able
> to accept the reproof, and a third that there was no one who
> knew how to administer reproof.[30]

He cites a testimony to the ability of Rabbi Akiba to receive reproof, even after four or five complaints, "For all
that, I know that he loved me the more."

Such a number of complaints may surprise us, but it
was taught that the number of admonitions should continue until the offender violently repulses you or positively
refuses to hear you; but the admonition must be carried
out in all kindness, and never put him to open shame.
Whoever makes his neighbor white with shame before
others is as if he shed blood, for to put one's fellow to an
open shame is counted one of the gravest sins. Such a
person has no share in the world to come and is as bad
as an adulterer or one who has nullified the covenant by
removing the marks of circumcision.[31]

In the book of Proverbs a warning is given not to reprove a scoffer or a wicked man, for the only return for
that will be hatred, but "reprove a wise man, and he will
love you" (ch. 9:8). Perhaps the highest point reached in

Judaism on this teaching is found in the Testament of Gad, who tells his readers to remove hatred from their hearts and to love each other in deed, word, and thought. After repeating the admonition to "love each other from the heart," the writer deals with the possibility of sin. If a man sins against you, you are to reply peaceably and not allow guile to enter your soul. Should the sinner repent and confess, he is to be forgiven without further ado. If he deny it with an oath, the reader is counseled not to wrangle, lest sin be doubled thereby. If he denys it and is shamed by the rebuke, he is to desist. However, if he is shameless and continues to sin, the only alternative left is to "even so forgive him from the heart, and leave the retribution to God" (Testament of Gad 6:1, 3–4,6a).

The discussion of humility was introduced into this context by later rabbis. Was it not more excellent to refrain from reproof altogether out of humility, since in admonishing another a man seems to assume superior righteousness himself? Prior to the New Testament era, however, this was not a problem.

Even among the Hellenistic philosophers the practice of rebuke was standard procedure, although it certainly had a nonreligious dimension. When one philosopher was told by a heckler what a scoundrel and fool he was, his reply was that his heckler obviously didn't know him very well or else he would have criticized him much more fully and sharply!

The New Testament uses the term *elenchō* only in a religious sense. It always means to confront someone with his sin and to invite him to turn from it. According to Matt. 18:15, Jesus himself instructed his disciples on the necessity of this rebuke and the form it was to take. With keen psychological insight, this pattern concentrates on that which estranges from God and our fellowmen. Not every nonconformist conduct is to be censured, but if your brother *sins*, then it is your responsibility to do something about it.[32] The responsibility is defined as "Go, reprove him, between you and him alone." It is doubtful that the RSV translation "tell" does justice to the original, whereas the NEB "go and take the matter up with him" seems too weak. Certainly Luther's "go punish him" is too strong. Perhaps Bauer's rendering, "show him his fault while you are alone with him," strikes the meaning as well as any. Clearly the assumption is that it is the responsibility of the observer to point out the matter to the sinner, in love. The privacy protects the "sinner" from exposure and shame and also gives him an opportunity to respond to the admonition in any way that he wishes. The instruction seems to anticipate a wholesome outcome, for "if he listens to you, you have gained your brother."

Underlying this pattern of admonition is the conviction that men should be made aware of their rebellion if ever they are to find their way to forgiveness. As Paul Minear puts it: "Awareness of rebellion is an occasion not for despair, but for hope." He cites the words of George Fox, who describes his counsel to a man in despair:

I told him that which showed him his sins, and troubled him for them, would show him his salvation; for he that shows a man his sin is the same that takes it away.[33]

In a similar vein Seward Hiltner has noted that

to be "convicted of sin" is ultimately good rather than bad news, for unless something transcending oneself had been operative, one could not realize he was convicted. But the road to conviction of sin is through understanding and love, not through denunciation.[34]

If he does not listen, then the matter takes on more serious proportions. Because you may be misguided in your understanding of what sin is or because you may be wrongly motivated, the encounter with the brother takes on semilegal form. By taking one or two brothers with you, you have made available witnesses to testify to the attitude taken by the erring brother.[35]

The third and final step involves treating him like a Gentile or a tax collector, i.e., beginning to deal with the man as a nonmember and treating him as an object for evangelism.

It should be clear from this and a study of the context of Matt., ch. 18, that the purpose of this whole process is the attainment of forgiveness. Although the original situation in life is obscure and there are those who raise legitimate questions about the genuineness of this saying, its presence in Matthew shows us beyond doubt how one part of the primitive church understood the teachings of Jesus about forgiveness. The whole chapter deals with entrance into the Kingdom, how to treat those who have newly become members (the "little ones"), and the importance of each individual even when he falls into sin or strays (vs. 12 f.). The forgiving presence of Christ is promised to those who gather in his name ("two or three"), and Peter's question: "How often am I to forgive my brother?" (vs. 21–22) and the parable all contribute to this point. The importance of "forgiving your brother from the heart" (v. 35) also is a part of this total pattern and, in fact, forms the sum of the matter.

CORPORATE ADMONITION

In addition to this pattern of private rebuke, it seems that the purpose of the worship experience was not merely to make people feel better but, more important, to enable them to encounter Christ in a moving and significant way. For the unbeliever or outsider who came to a Christian service of worship, it was deemed most important that he understand what was going on. Paul observes in one of his letters that if the members of the church are babbling in tongues, the unbeliever will conclude that the Christians are mad. If, however, they are speaking an intelligible language,

the visitor, when he enters, hears from everyone something that searches his conscience and brings conviction [*elenchō*], and the secrets of his heart are laid bare. So he will fall down and worship God, crying, "God is certainly among you!" (I Cor. 14:24 f., NEB).

The word Paul uses here for judgment (*anakrinō*) is one that has a legal connotation. It would seem that Paul sees the assemblies at Corinth as having this kind of purpose. Just as the Samaritan woman was convinced that if Jesus could lay his finger on her sin, he must be the prophet (John, ch. 4), so Paul assumes that the Christian church will attract others and move them to the conviction that God really has his dwelling among them if they can reveal the secrets of their heart and bring about a conviction of sin. Prior to the cure comes the diagnosis. Prior to forgiveness comes recognition of sin. For the early church, this meant reproof and rebuke after judgment had taken place.

Closely related to this bringing about of a conviction is the practice of admonition, instruction, and warning that seems to center around the pastoral task. The Greek word, *nouthesia*, which designates this function, is confined to Pauline literature but has a rich history in earlier Greek literature. Literally, it means to "place in the mind, heart, or affections." Socrates, e.g., wishes to take aside the educator who unintentionally made an error, in order to instruct him and warn him. In teaching (*didaskō*), the stress seems to fall upon the intellect, whereas admonition aims at a response in the realm of the emotions and the will and presupposes a degree of resistance that has to be overcome. The mind is progressing in a bad direction and therefore needs to be straightened. That which is false needs correction and the unhealthy or unsound attitude removed. Earnestness and seriousness pervade this process. As compared with teaching, Debrunner states that teaching shows how something is to be done, whereas admonition shows what has been done wrongly.[36]

In the New Testament it is used in connection with the family situation; fathers are urged to "give their children instruction and the correction which belongs to Christian education" (Eph. 6:4). The Old Testament Scriptures are said to have been written for our warning (I Cor. 10:11).

For the rest, the term "admonition" (*nouthesia*) is almost exclusively used as an aspect of pastoral care. Paul, in his farewell address to the Ephesian elders, reminds them that for three years he did not cease to admonish them night and day with tears (Acts 20:31).[37] To admonish each one individually fits in with the description of Paul's work among the Colossians, whom he said he admonished and taught individually without distinction (Col. 1:28). Likewise, he seeks to bring the Corinthians to their senses through admonition but without any desire to shame them (I Cor. 4:14). Paul thinks of himself as a Jewish rabbi thought of his pupils, as their father (v. 15), and he seems to blend both the tenderness of a mother's care (I Thess. 2:7) and the more active role of the father in "exhorting, encouraging, and charging them to lead a life worthy of God" (vs. 11 f.).

The fact that some are called "the ones admonishing" would seem to indicate that Paul saw this as primarily a pastoral task (ch. 5:12). On the other hand, in three churches he urges that the task of mutual admonition not be neglected. To the Romans he indicates that he has confidence that they have been enabled to carry on the task of mutual admonition (Rom. 15:14). He urges the Colossians to allow the word of Christ to dwell among them richly as they teach and admonish each other in all wisdom (Col. 3:16). The Thessalonians are urged especially to admonish the idle (I Thess. 5:14) and to admonish as they would a brother the one who refuses to listen to Paul's letters (II Thess. 3:15). In the admonition in Titus 3:10 that the factious man is to be left alone after one or two admonitions, we may see a reflection of the instructions found in Matt., ch. 18. The pattern of admonition is not to continue indefinitely.

In all these instances, including the last, we must see admonition as a step in the direction of the experience of forgiveness. Admonition is necessary because of the continuing presence of sin in the church. Even more, it is called forth because it is unnecessary to tolerate sin in the church since the victory of Christ over sin, and impossible for the church ever to settle down with it. Church discipline does not have a punitive function but a redemptive one. The shepherd's aim is to rescue the sheep from those forces which will destroy it or to warn of those dangers that lurk unknown to the sheep.

Each epistle in the New Testament is a fruit of this process of admonition. Each is meant to prevent the church from slipping back into the mire of sin and darkness from which its members have been so recently rescued. Each is meant to strengthen the foundations of the church as it moves against the forces of evil that seek to slay it.

Seen in this context, discipline is not a bit of optional equipment that the church may or may not possess as it chooses. It belongs to the very essence of community life, where each man is his brother's keeper and each is willing to allow the log to be removed from his own eye as well as to assist in removing the speck from his brother's. If discipline is practiced in the context of forgiveness and with no other aim than to achieve forgiveness, perhaps it could be restored to its rightful place in contemporary Protestantism. Because sin is corporate and because salvation is corporate, the church cannot be the church without finding the means to deal with sin within the societal or interpersonal relations of its members.[38]

CHAPTER XII

Psychiatric Dimensions of Forgiveness

In a study of the dynamics of Christian forgiveness, it is not only inadvisable but impossible to avoid a discussion of forgiveness in psychiatry. From the outset, however, such a discussion encounters some problems. Does psychiatry as a science have any place for a term so freighted with theological tradition? When it occurs in psychiatric literature, is it to be seen as a relic of the writer's religious background or as an attempt to use a theological term for a psychological process? The possibility that the term "forgiveness" is simply a part of the common baggage of Western culture, where it has played a significant role, cannot be ruled out. Nevertheless, since psychiatry has for the most part followed Freud's lead in "representing the sense of guilt as the most important problem in the development of civilization,"[1] it is not surprising to note that the term "forgiveness" figures in its literature. Our interest is in noting the similarities and differences between the Biblical and psychiatric perspectives on forgiveness.

In Sigmund Freud's writings, the idea of forgiveness is found scarcely at all. Indeed, it would seem that he rejects the Christian conception of God as being too lenient and too kind. He seems to prefer a more strict and demanding father image than Christianity or Judaism have to offer.[2] Nevertheless, in an illuminating reference to forgiveness in a letter (1928) to the Protestant pastor, Oskar Pfister, he states that the utterance, "Thy sins are forgiven thee; arise and walk" is "psychologically profound." In his attempt to analyze the statement he catches the scandal involved in it:

If the sick man had asked: "how knowest thou that my sins are forgiven?" the answer could only have been: "I, the Son of God, forgive thee." In other words, a call for unlimited transference. And now, just suppose I said to a patient: "I, Professor Sigmund Freud, forgive thee thy sins," what a fool I would make of myself.[3]

What is remarkable is that Freud recognizes the psychological value of the declaration of forgiveness. Yet the audacity of it repels him. The same objection had already been raised by the contemporaries of Jesus and has been raised all too often in the church.

In a later letter (1930) Pfister returns to a basic tension that he sees between psychoanalysis and Christianity on the doctrine of revenge and sacrifice, for which Christianity substitutes the principle of love and forgiveness. This he describes as one of the "big new problems." He sees the need for retribution as it has been elucidated in Freud's recent works, and he has little trouble with the practice of sacrifice. In regard, however, to the "genuinely Christian doctrine of forgiveness" as seen in the parable of the prodigal son,

there is obviously a regression to the childhood state in which the child is not treated by the standard of good and evil, but simply with love and kindness. However that does not solve the real problem. The application of the principle of retribution or forgiveness is among the most difficult things in education. We always have to set up rules, which leads to all sorts of trouble, until we are forced to overthrow the rules and return to the original intention. Is there not analytic action in all acts of grace and forgiveness?[4]

It would seem that the tension between psychoanalysis and the Christian experience of forgiveness is here seen correctly. One senses an almost wistful query, for Pfister felt that it could not be that psychoanalysis, which had thrown so much light on the nature of the human problem, was at variance with Christianity on the issue of forgiveness. Neither Freud nor Pfister, however, allowed the problem to become oversimplified, and in so doing probably helped the discussion between religion and psychiatry in the long run. Freud seems at least to have clearly detected the distance between himself and a member of the church who, under the authority of Christ, declares to another that his sins are forgiven.

One of Freud's most faithful followers, Otto Fenichel, has made extensive use of the word "forgiveness" to describe some of the dynamics of human experience. In his theory the ego needs some degree of absolution from the superego and has a variety of ways of achieving this. Particularly as the need for punishment develops,

the pressure from the part of the super-ego to which the ego is exposed creates first of all a need for getting rid of the lost self-esteem, and for reassurance against possible feelings of annihilation. This aim is best achieved by "forgiveness." After the experience that punishment may actually develop. The punishment longed for is a means of achieving forgiveness; the individuals in question certainly would prefer it if they could achieve forgiveness without first undergoing punishment."[5]

According to this theory, the superego does the forgiving or, better, the ego works out its own forgiveness with fear and trembling. Forgiveness is an inner psychic phenomenon that does not involve an external agent. It is certainly not to be denied that the need for punishment has at times been at work in certain attempts to acquire forgiveness. The question is whether we are rooted in the Biblical view of forgiveness when it is visualized as such.

There will be those who are uneasy about letting the Freudian school have the only word to speak for psychiatry. Historically, it has, of course, said the first word and probably still speaks the most important word. Yet when we widen our scope of inquiry, the picture does not change materially, although the issues change somewhat. One question that now emerges is whether acceptance in psychiatric literature and practice is to be equated with forgiveness. Paul Tillich has taken the position that "being forgiven and being able to accept one's self are one and the same things."[6] Against this, some strong objections have been raised. These objections undoubtedly center not only on the way in which acceptance has been cheapened by constant usage but also on the realization that behind it lies what seems to many to be a shallow conception of human relations. What does it mean "to accept someone"? As nearly as we can tell, what is meant is that we approach people just as they are, without passing prior judgment on them because of color of skin or outward behavior. The person is accepted as such, and every attempt is made to avoid censoriousness that might alienate the client from us. I listen with interest to what he has to say, perhaps even with a certain degree of empathy or sympathy. I relate to him just as he is without assuming that he shares my values or I share his. I do not

nurture the hope that I will be able to remake him according to what I think he can become.

On the surface, it must be admitted that such a description of relating to people stands in no fundamental conflict with the gospel. No wonder we often hear people
say that Jesus accepted the sinners and that Paul en-
couraged the Romans to accept one another even as Christ
has accepted us (Rom. 15:7, NEB).

It would seem to be rather clear that there can be no
forgiveness without acceptance. Acceptance is the open-
ing act that makes it possible for people to relate to each
other. It certainly can be asserted that the church should
be accepting and should learn to relate to new people and
especially to people who stand under the censure of society and their own consciences.

Whereas, then, it is impossible to be forgiving without
being accepting, it is quite possible to be accepting without knowing about forgiveness or caring to know anything
about it. To speak of forgiveness, we must assume the
presence of sin.

It is quite clear that psychiatry has two positions here.
On the one hand Albert Ellis contends that

giving anyone a sense of sin, guilt or self-blame is the worst
possible way to help him to be an emotionally sound and
adequately socialised individual . . . . If . . . we can teach our
patients . . . that even though human beings can be held quite
accountable or responsible for their misdeeds, no one is ever
to blame for anything, human morality will be significantly
improved . . . . The concept of sin is the direct and indirect
cause of virtually all neurotic disturbance. The sooner psycho-
therapists forthrightly begin to attack it the better their patients will be.[7]

Although this is a direct statement, it should not be assumed that Ellis speaks only for himself. Many feel this

way, and most assume that the category of "sin" does not belong in therapy, although it can be discussed by the clergy. Wherever such a position prevails it is clear that talking about forgiveness is meaningless, because no sin is assumed. We might better talk of tolerance or indifference or excusing. As already observed, Mowrer takes a quite different position, but he appears to be addressing himself to the clergy as much as to his fellow therapists. As ministers, we have tended to neglect the healing aspects of judgment. We must allow the healing process of judgment to take its place in the dynamics of forgiveness. None of this is to be confused with tolerance or excusing, because they operate on completely different levels.[8] There has been a good deal of sympathy for the maxim "To understand everything is to forgive everything" among the psychiatric technicians. The folly of such an approach would seem best demonstrated in the case of the tyrants (such as Hitler) or the assassins, where to understand means to condemn almost everything. Forgiveness is only possible where responsibility is taken seriously and where repentance is evidence of this responsibility.[9] Any discussion of forgiveness in psychiatry must therefore take seriously the difference that exists between psychiatry and Biblical literature on this point. We cannot avoid asking whether we are even justified in speaking of forgiveness in psychiatry without qualification or even substitution.[10]

This does not mean that what happens to a person under psychiatric care may not have profound meaning and radical consequences, even in his understanding of forgiveness. The psychiatrist who sees his role as a member of the church, with the conviction that he is one priest among many, certainly should not hesitate to see himself as an agent of divine forgiveness, even though it may not be prudent to advertise himself as such. Fundamentally, it would seem that only he who sees forgiveness as rooted in the nature of a forgiving God, and he who sees himself as representing that God, should speak of forgiveness. Otherwise, human experience will be greatly impoverished by the shallow conception of forgiveness that already circulates so widely. Christian forgiveness has deep historical roots focused most sharply in the life, death, and resurrection of Jesus Christ, and any discussion of forgiveness apart from that will tend to inflate the term even more than it has already been inflated. The fact that the church has tended to stress the theological dimension of forgiveness at the expense of the psychological should not cause us now to jettison the theological side altogether.

One example of a psychiatrist who has recognized the importance of both sides of this is Andras Angyal. He observed that a patient usually comes to a psychiatrist "not to *be* better, but simply to *feel* better . . . . In a way he wishes to learn how to sin without being punished for it."[11] The evidence that repentance has taken place has to go deeper than the mere fact that he is seeing a psychiatrist. Angyal sees repentance as the most important step in the admission of the futility of the unhealthy pattern. The second step that marks the way out he calls "insight" in psychiatric terms and "forgiveness" in theological terms. There is much good material in his attempt to relate these two concepts. His views that one needs a fulcrum outside of oneself in order to lift a burden, and that one cannot lift oneself by one's own bootstraps, both agree with Biblical religion. Angyal himself describes forgiveness thus:

Beyond being a mere interpreter, the therapist exercises a more important influence upon the progress of recovery through his attitude toward the patient, through the spirit in which his

interpretations are given. The patient notices that the thera-
peutist [*sic!*] does not blame him; he gradually notices also that
the unpunitive attitude of the therapist is not based on a
moral indifference. The therapist takes seriously the unwhole-
some attitudes and behavior of the patient, in some ways more
seriously than the patient himself, because he perceives more
clearly their destructiveness. In spite, however, of seeing the
shortcomings of the patient in all their seriousness, the therapist continues to value his patient as a person and shows sincere respect toward him. . . . Thus the patient becomes aware
that within his own self there is something else, something that
is different and is outside of his neurotic way of life. He now
has within himself a fulcrum that is outside of the neurotic
enclosure.

I believe that what I have described in the last paragraph
corresponds point by point to the religious concept of *forgiveness*. Obviously this basic concept means neither abstaining
from retaliation, nor does it mean a superficial "let's forget
about it," nor is it a meaningless statement that "no harm has
been done." The true act of forgiving has a negative and a
positive aspect, it implies a denial and an assertion. The negative aspect consists in recognizing the unhealthy, ill-motivated
behavior as such straightforwardly, yet not considering this
behavior as indicative of what the person really is in his deepest self. This negative aspect is a forgiving in the sense of
giving away, removing, unveiling, as if one puts aside a mask
which is not organically a part of the person. The positive
aspect of forgiving consists in revealing, in making apparent
the real worth, the real nucleus of the person. In religious
parlance one would express this by saying that in the act of
forgiving one sees the person outwardly as a sinner and
inwardly as a child of God.[12]

Angyal is certainly correct when he observes that forgiveness is not a single dramatic event but a laborious
translation, item by item. He is also correct in relating the
forgiving work of the therapist with the process of forgiving as it begins to operate in the patient, who must begin

by forgiving his therapist and then move on to wider horizons of forgiveness. The profoundly liberating dimensions of such an experience extend, then, not only to the neurotic structures of the individual but also have repercussions in his dealings with others. All in all, Angyal represents one of the most competent statements of the areas of convergence between religion and psychotherapy in the area of forgiveness.

Forgiving Is Not Forgetting

One of the most serious mistakes the church has made is to equate forgiving and forgetting. It is true, of course, that to claim to have forgiven someone and then to remind him periodically of his sin makes a mockery of forgiveness. Likewise, however, the assumption that sins once committed can by sheer effort of human or divine will be forgotten is naïve and can burden people with even more guilt, because they cannot forget something as they concentrate on trying to do so! In this area we have much to learn from the behavioral disciplines. He who tries to cut himself off from the past has no future. It is the nature of repentance that it makes the past remain nothing but the *past*. It means to cut yourself off from those elements of the past which seek your destruction and deny them power over you for the present. For in all of us, the elements of the past, consisting of both curse and blessing, struggle for dominance. On this conflict Paul Tillich has written some perceptive words:

A pathetic struggle with their past is going on almost without interruption in many men and women in our time. No medical healing can solve *this* conflict, because no medical healing can change the past. Only a blessing and curse can heal; it is the blessing which changes what seems to be unchangeable—the past. It cannot change the facts: what has happened has happened and remains so in all eternity! But the *meaning* of the facts can be changed by the eternal, and the name of this change is the experience of "forgiveness." If the meaning of the past is changed by forgiveness, its influence on the future is also changed. The character of curse is taken away from it. It has become a blessing by the transforming power of forgiveness.[13]

Forgiveness, then, is not forgetting. It is allowing the past to lose its sting and its curse, freeing us for joyful service in spite of dismal failures in the past. Such a change is a direct attack on the root of the human problem. It does not satisfy itself with soothing placebos or narcotic agents. It is a change that has its origin in God himself and thus provides opportunities beyond the merely human resources that are in man.

The church's point that forgiving is forgetting has had a strong side. On occasion, people say that they are tired of forgiving. They tell you that for ten or fifteen years they have tried to be forgiving with their partner in business or in marriage, but now they are tired of that approach and they are going to try a different one. As you listen to these people over a longer period of time, you discover that they have in fact not been forgiving at all. Indeed, they have perfected the art of remembering every little injustice done to them. Every insult is vividly etched in their memories. To be sure, one should allow them the option of trying a different approach. However, to assume that they have been forgiving and that now they are going to assert themselves and insist on their rights is folly. What they have been doing is preparing their case for one fatal act of destruction, all the time deceiving themselves that they are forgiving. Their failure to forgive is made most obvious in their desire now to even the score.[14]

On occasion, however, the pastor and counselor has a situation in which he has to face the problem squarely: for the sake of the good of all concerned, should not forgiveness yield to nonforgiveness? The Christian has a delicate problem on his hand, for his call to forgiveness is patterned upon that of the Lord's forgiveness of him, and he cannot, therefore, ever call a halt. The seventy times seven means infinity and is consciously patterned in contrast to Cain's sevenfold vengeance described in Gen. 4:24. Yet he needs at every point to be clear that what is operating is truly Christian forgiveness or else the harvest that he reaps may instead be one of sorrow. What seems clear is that where people have claimed to be fed up with forgiving and have tried retaliation, their joy has not increased proportionately, and there is evidence to indicate that they are in fact among the most miserable people in the world. Little wonder, for they have reverted back to the most elementary law of nature, the law of retaliation, which is as destructive in human affairs as it is in nature.

In the popular press, one occasionally finds testimonials to the superiority of the alternate approach. One woman writes from her own experience that "a wife can't ever forget [even though she may forgive] a husband's unfaithfulness," but also that "to seek revenge is meaningless."[15] Abigail Van Buren relates that she once published a letter beginning: "If there is a reader somewhere who has caught her husband being unfaithful, has forgiven him, and has since had a happy marriage, would you please ask her to tell her story?" which was followed by a swift and overwhelming response. Many of the answering letters had the same message: "The rewards of forgiveness, the futility of harboring a grudge." On forgiveness, many said that "it wasn't easy to forget." Throughout all the letters ran the theme: "Forgive and forget." They were a striking testimony to the power of love and forgiveness. One respondent wrote: "You will never know, unless you do both, pray and forgive seventy times seven, what a grand and glorious feeling it is to rise above the hurt."[16] To those who object to such simple statements of human experience one could reply that this is valid data, drawn from human experience, entitled to a hearing in the total discussion of the meaning of forgiveness.

What we have said is that psychiatry began with an attitude toward forgiveness different from that taken by the church. Its use of the term "acceptance" does not designate what the church means by forgiveness. Psychiatry has taught us something about the extent to which one can forget the past and that we need to find a better formula than "forgiving is forgetting." Wherever forgiveness remains grounded in God's forgiveness of us, it has great power for human relationships, which we have every reason to proclaim with boldness. We should realize that the alternatives to forgiveness are so destructive that they should not be seriously contemplated. Above all, it may be said that no words have as much healing power for individual and corporate ills as the two words, "I'm sorry."[17]

Beyond this, however, it should be stressed again that the Biblical emphasis is not so much on forgiveness as on reconciliation.[18] Forgiveness, then, is merely the prelude to reconciliation. The process of reconciliation may be a long one indeed, but it is certain that it will never be accomplished unless there is first of all acceptance on one side of the conflict, and a willingness to forgive and then to be reconciled. Hitherto unknown depths of fellowship are available to people who have forgiven and been forgiven and experienced the joys of reconciliation.

A wrong forgiven does normally and naturally deepen as well as confirm the mutual knowledge of persons. Forgiveness does not only forestall or remove enmity: it strengthens love. Thus the consummation of forgiveness implies and demands a desire on both sides that a wrong done whether it can be undone or not shall be deprived of its power to alienate.[19]

In fact, it may well be that as we become reconciled to each other we experience what Jacob did when he was reconciled to his brother Esau: "Truly to see your face is like seeing the face of God" (Gen. 33:10).

Is There Such a Thing as Self-forgiveness?

Protestant theology has been plagued by the idea that man can forgive himself. When man was at the center of the stage, even of the study of theology, it is not too surprising to have the idea emerge that man's biggest problem is that he cannot forgive himself. Paul Lehmann says that in regard to Ritschl, the most appropriate critical superscription with which to adorn the portals of Ritschl's theological reconstruction is, "Man wants forgiveness: and man forgives himself." The peculiar combination of psychology and theology in the nineteenth century made it easy for forgiveness to be seen primarily in terms of self-forgiveness. Abetting this process was the tendency to see sin primarily as ignorance rather than as rebellion.[20]

With the Barthian revolution, all this has been changed. The Barthian theology has its own dangers, but it is not the danger of allowing forgiveness to be carried on by man. Barth's influence has been pervasive in Europe, but in this country its influence has been relatively small, especially in the area of pastoral care. Among those influenced by Barth, there is agreement on the central issue that forgiveness constitutes in Protestantism. The excellent book on pastoral care written by Barth's close co-worker, Eduard Thurneysen, places forgiveness at the center of the pastoral task.

The content of the proclamation of pastoral care can be no other than the forgiveness of sins through Jesus Christ. God's absolving grace must be communicated in pastoral care . . . . The power of forgiveness consists precisely in the fact that man is reclaimed for God, in body and soul, and brought under his hand, just as truly as sin seized his whole existence down to its last psychophysical depths. True pastoral care does not rest until it has carried the forgiving Word into these depths in the strength of the Spirit and of prayer and has really and completely brought man again under the healing power of grace.[21]

Theology clearly maintains its integrity here, and God remains God! Anyone acquainted with the mainstream of pastoral psychology will lay Thurneysen's book down with some questions about the way in which forgiveness becomes a psychologically meaningful experience and how the pastor contributes to the dynamics of the process. Little help comes from Thurneysen at this point.

The lack of psychological interest on the part of the Biblical writers should not mislead us into believing that they are uninterested in what happens in the human experience. They are not charting psychological processes, because they are more interested in describing what happens in the God-man encounter from their perspective, which is not a modern one (which certainly does not mean it is out of date!). The efforts of Barth and Thurneysen to maintain the integrity of the Biblical position have much to say to us. We cannot allow the dynamics of human experience to mesmerize us into believing that this is the sum and substance of experience. Forgiveness, however, offers an excellent example, because it is an experience rooted in God but running its course within human experience.[22] Thus the Barthian insistence on the dialectic, polar nature of forgiveness would seem right. We cannot forgive ourselves, but it is *we* who are forgiven. I cannot forgive myself, but you as a member of the church can forgive me. Forgiveness occurs, however, only as you yourself participate in the power of God to forgive and as you allow that power to work through you. Guilt is then conquered by grace.

CHAPTER XIII

Forgiveness and the Pastoral Task

We hear a good deal today about the group ministry and about the ministry of the laity:

By all means in his power, the preacher of the Word must help men to understand that forgiveness, freely offered in the Gospel; but above all, he must help them to take it, as in the grace of God he has taken it himself.[1]

Such words are indigenous to the Protestant Reformation, and those who have been set apart to proclaim the gospel and have taken years of training to teach it in the churches should warmly welcome such developments. Let the whole people of God be drawn into the great work to be done in the church, for no special class, no matter how dedicated and well-trained, can do all the work. There will always be a need for leadership roles in the church and there will always be a need for special training, whether it is in counseling, the teaching and preaching of the Word, or whatever it may be.

Because of this special ministry, a consideration of the peculiar challenge faced by the Protestant ministry seems in order. How does the task of the pastor relate to the Christian dynamics of forgiveness? How can he relate every activity to this goal of helping people to achieve forgiveness in their lives?[2]

First, he must himself be convinced that it is important. Nothing is to be gained by trying to make it the sum and substance of his message; on the other hand, he cannot ignore the fact that powerful guilt-inducing factors are at work in our culture to which he must relate himself. He can add to these factors, and there must be times when he does so. Most often, the best way to do so is to present such a strong case for a life of victory and courage that people find their condemnation by comparison. Iago says of Cassio, "He hath a daily beauty in his life that makes me ugly." This is what Simon Peter experienced when he hauled in the fish and said to Christ: "Depart from me, for I am a sinful man" (Luke 5:8), for that is the way he felt after he met Christ. We do not see the dreadfulness of our sin until after we have come to forgiveness. As Karl Barth says: "Sin scorches us when it comes under the light of forgiveness, not before. Sin scorches us then by becoming visible as our enmity against God."[3]

There is no excuse for a sermon to be guilt-inducing if at the same time it does not clearly point to a way of release. In fact, it may be that the best way to confront the sin question is always to do so obliquely. Judgment is a part of the Christian gospel, and it belongs to part of the task of the minister, but it may never in this life be divorced from God's offer of forgiveness.

Whenever the minister addresses himself to the subject of guilt and forgiveness, the emphasis must be placed on God's forgiveness as demonstrated to us in the life of Jesus Christ. It is significant that since Celsus there have always been voices raised against the church's message of forgiveness. Recently, O. Hobart Mowrer, a psychologist by profession, has chided the clergy for speaking so much of forgiveness. He considers forgiveness

as something of an anachronism: it is inadequate or else it is unnecessary. And clergymen take an awesome responsibility upon themselves when they begin to traffic in this questionable commodity.[4]

Seen from his vantage point, forgiveness is a "letting him off easy," and therefore he places a good deal of stress on restitution and public confession of wrongs. He prefers that we talk about sin rather than sickness, urging Protestant churches to "reconsider the institution of confession, stress restitution and reform, not forgiveness."[5]

What Mowrer has to say about confession and restitution has psychological value. What he has to say about sin and forgiveness is not only shallow and unknowledgeable but actually dangerous. It is the more dangerous because Protestant ministers have an inherent tendency to look with respect upon anyone who speaks from the behavioral sciences, especially when he confirms them in their prejudices. Our greatest danger in listening to Mowrer is to be misled into the simplistic definition of sin that he offers us. According to him, it would seem that every petty violation is a sin. The deeper level of sin as estrangement and disobedience toward God, in prideful rebellion against God, is not grasped. How confess that? How make restitution for that?

Mowrer speaks, he says, as an empirical scientist and cannot be bothered with the theological adequacy of his formulas. Yet he does not hesitate to say what he thinks the church should say about this or that problem, nor does he hesitate in stating what he thinks the clergy ought to be doing about this or that. His definition of sin seems primarily sexually oriented, thus betraying perhaps either a much greater debt to Freud than he wants to allow or a lesser degree of emancipation from his childhood conscience than one might expect. He can see only the weaknesses of the Freudian approach, yet makes the same fundamental error Freud made. As Freud exalted one therapeutic technique until his followers believed it could help everyone, so Mowrer lauds one therapeutic technique because it has helped him. Must "scientists" always fall victims to this temptation to universalize on their own experience?

Not only does Mowrer suffer from a totally inadequate view of sin, but he also grossly misunderstands what the church means by forgiveness.[6] Surely forgiveness has never been understood as undoing the past or as allowing someone to get off easily. It is precisely because no violation of justice can be allowed that Christ needed to suffer. Just as we today continue to bear the sufferings of our fellowmen as we comprise the body of Christ, the church, so no forgiveness is possible without suffering. Forgiveness, then, is not a commodity that we peddle or traffic in, but an experience that is so profound in its change in human personality that it defies the tools with which Mowrer works.

We could naturally adopt some schemes of confession and restitution. For a time they would "work." People do feel better when they talk about their failures and mistakes. However, such an approach when it lacks the dimension of divine forgiveness can soon become a spiritual nudist colony in which we allow our exhibitionist tendencies free play. We cannot earn our own salvation through

confession and restitution, all the while considering ourselves Christians. Furthermore, much as it may be re-
sented, there is a dimension of forgiveness, which if lost,
cuts out its heart. Who are you to forgive sins? implies that
you have some authority, either conferred upon you from
some external source or inherent by virtue of your experience, to confer forgiveness upon others. This is why the
church is a natural place in which forgiveness should be
attainable. The church is comprised of people who themselves have had a profound experience of the miracle of
forgiveness.[7]

SHOULD PROTESTANTISM HAVE A CONFESSIONAL?

Every Protestant pastor has with some envy considered
the Roman Catholic confessional. At times we try to reassure ourselves by saying that many Roman Catholics
don't really take the confessional seriously anyway and
that they have as much trouble with guilt as we do.

Yet in our more objective moments we remember that
Luther had high praise for the practice of mutual confession. Our experience leads us to agree with Adolf von
Harnack's opinion that Protestantism didn't like the rotten
fruit (the abuses of the confessional) and so cut down the
tree.[8] Whether we restore the confessional or not, it seems
crystal clear that if Protestantism is to survive with any
significance, it will need to find more adequate ways of
dealing with guilt than it has found so far. There are, in
fact, pastors who are experimenting with public confession; others have considered their counseling sessions as
confessional experiences. In some groups the public confession of sins is still practiced regularly.[9]

Experience has taught us that any public confession of
sins is open to serious abuses. So are love and the home,

but we do not therefore discontinue them. Yet the abuses of the public confession of sins can be overcome. It is clear that not everyone has the maturity to receive the confession of sins. There must then be a sifting of people who have the moral strength to receive a confession of sins. Ideally, every member of the church ought to have this strength, but one notices that even the churches which have stressed most responsible church membership have been aware that not all of their members have the strength to receive the confession of sins from their brothers.

In each case of public confession the pastor should help the member to think through the reasons why he feels he should make a public confession. There may be self-destructive tendencies at work in the desire to make the confession, and these should be worked through. These same forces may have been at work in the original act, and to allow them to complete their demonic work in this fashion is not our mandate.

Similar considerations must guide us in the question of restitution. Very few sins can be "restored," but in those cases where it is possible and the initiative lies with the guilty party the church should not stand in the way. In certain cases where sums of money have been stolen and could not be returned to the offended party, equal sums have been given to community organizations. As in the case of confession, it must be clearly pointed out to the people involved that there can be no question of *earning* forgiveness. Our acts bear witness to the fact that we have been forgiven; they do not accomplish forgiveness. Restitution must always have a very modest place in the dynamics of forgiveness for this reason. We dare not even see our life under Christ and for our fellowmen as a way of making amends. It is love's response to love revealed and should be a life of joyful gratitude to God for all that he did for us in Jesus Christ. The only drivenness in the gospel is that of gratitude.

It would seem, then, that there are valid reasons for trying to allow the kind of community to develop in which our burdens are borne by one another. In larger churches it may be possible to form contract groups in which mutual trust and confidence are built. Here the church can learn much from group therapy. However, the church must always be wary of allowing itself to see its mission as a prying agency in which the intimacy of private life is invaded. The church must have avenues available in which the burdened soul can find forgiveness, but it must not force its gift of freedom and release from sin upon those not asking for it. Above all, the church values each individual because of the gift that the Holy Spirit has given to him or her and seeks, therefore, to help that person to give and receive from its total life that which God wills. The group that is a part of the church must be a binding and loosing group. It takes a contract upon itself and seeks to keep that contract, but there are times when the contract is broken, and all that can then be done is to forgive. The loosing function is extremely important. Here we dare not hide behind the false modesty: "Who am I to forgive sins?" for when we do, we negate the incarnation.

CAN I SPEAK WORDS OF ABSOLUTION?

Many ministers have no great difficulty declaring forgiveness from the pulpit and reading the words of absolution in an order of service, but they find it more difficult to do so in private or even in a small group. This is strange in view of the clarity of the mandate Christ gave his disciples. May not, in fact, this be where our greatest breakdown lies? Some say, "They are 'merely' words, why speak them?" Such a position underestimates the power of the word. Psychotherapy has certainly confirmed what is already clear in Biblical thought: Words are effective carriers of great healing power. Of course they can also carry a lethal freight, but those who are ministers of the gospel know how great are the powers endued in the word. What kind of meaningful institution is available to the church today to assure its people of divine forgiveness? We have no annual atonement day, and many churches do not even have or use the absolution formula in their liturgy. Perhaps it does not belong there, for Jesus spoke only to individuals: "Your sins are forgiven you." At least, then, we must have it in the private consultations when confession is made to us and we speak that word which Christ has authorized us to speak: "Your sins are forgiven." The minister experiences some of the greatest joys of his work at that moment.[10] For he knows that when confession is made, a soul has turned itself toward God, and he can only do one thing—assure the penitent one that God has already turned to him and forgiven him. He can do no less than that, and he should do it clearly and forthrightly. Above all, he must work toward establishing a kind of community that by its tone and quality of life is a forgiving community.

What is striking about J. A. T. Robinson's significant book *Honest to God* is not its courage to ask radical questions but its lack of courage to follow through consistently on some of the evidence it presents. Robinson cites the experience of John Wren-Lewis who came to belief in a personal God "through the experience of discovering in a community 'the creative and "numinous" power' inherent in *ordinary* personal relationships." What Wren-Lewis discovered was actually an entirely different mode of living-in-relationship from anything known in the world, a *redeemed* mode of relationship in which the special energy Blake called "mutual forgiveness" operated in a way that made the professional "permissiveness" of the psychotherapist's consulting-room seem a pale shadow in comparison.[11]

John Wren-Lewis is not an isolated case. In the light of such a stirring testimony it is indeed strange that Robinson's critique of the church does not focus on the structure of its community life. Must we not have the courage to ask this radical question, knowing very well that it involves asking whether the hierarchy, liturgy, and traditional meeting forms may not, in fact, have outlived their usefulness? The problem in asking the tame questions, as Robinson does, is that no one is given any help on how a community of forgiveness is recovered. Not only traditional concepts of God need to be challenged, but the traditional structures of the church need to be reexamined to see whether the energy of forgiveness is now being effectively mediated to people through the activities of the church. That the church can be a community of forgiveness and has been at times in the past is clear. It has a long way to go, however, before many people like John Wren-Lewis will find in it a community of mutual forgiveness. Unless it goes that way, unless all its agencies and forms contribute to making it a community of forgiveness and reconciliation, it cannot be considered an authentic church. The words of absolution that we speak ring with hollowness unless they are backed by a people who have experienced forgiveness and have practiced the art of assisting others to find forgiveness.

Notes

INTRODUCTION

1. Charles Williams, *He Came Down from Heaven; and, The Forgiveness of Sins* (London: Faber & Faber, Ltd., 1950), p. 107.

2. H. R. Mackintosh, *The Christian Experience of Forgiveness* (first published London: James Nisbet & Co., Ltd., 1927, and often reprinted).

3. James G. Emerson, Jr., *The Dynamics of Forgiveness* (The Westminster Press, 1964), deliberately begins with people where they are and consequently never seriously attempts to arrive at a Biblical understanding of forgiveness (p. 27).

4. Joseph Haroutunian, "Grace and Freedom Reconsidered," *Journal of Religion*, Vol. XL (1960), p. 73.

5. Hans Hofmann, *Religion and Mental Health* (Harper & Row, Publishers, Inc., 1961), p. 30.

6. O. Hobart Mowrer, *The Crisis in Psychiatry and Religion* (D. Van Nostrand Company, Inc., 1961), pp. 77, 106.

7. Sigmund Freud, "An Outline of Psycho-Analysis," *International Journal of Psychoanalysis*, Vol. XXI (1940), p. 52.

8. "One works to the best of one's power, . . . as a father confessor who gives absolution, as it were, by a continuance of his sympathy and respect after the confession has been made." (Freud, *Studies on Hysteria*, SE, Vol. II, p. 282,

written about 1895.) Compare also Karl Menninger, *Theory of Psychoanalytic Technique* (Basic Books, Inc., Publishers, 1958), pp. 58, 71, 100; and J. Frank, *Persuasion and Healing* (The Johns Hopkins Press, 1961), p. 180 *et passim.*

CHAPTER I

1. This method is also used by J. J. Stamm, *Erlösen und Vergeben im Alten Testament* (Bern, 1940); E. B. Redlich, *The Forgiveness of Sins* (Edinburgh: T. & T. Clark, 1937), pp. 3–70; and by Sven Herner, *Sühne und Vergebung in Israel* (Lund, 1942). Walther Eichrodt, *Theologie des Alten Testaments,* Vols. II and III (Leipzig, 1939), pp. 81–141, uses a thematic approach. For a recent summary of the Old Testament material, see C. J. de Catanzaro, "Forgiveness in the Old Testament," *American Church Quarterly,* Vol. II (1962), pp. 26–39.

2. So H.-J. Kraus, *Psalmen* (Neukirchen Kreis Moers, 1960), Vol. II, p. 599.

3. See Stamm, *op. cit.,* pp. 67 ff.

4. For discussions of this verse, see Kraus, *op. cit.,* Vol. II, p. 871, and Stamm, *op. cit.,* pp. 137 ff., who concludes, "Through forgiveness freely granted Jahweh obtains new children of his glory and thereby new subjects who honor him."

5. For evidence that the rabbis did not follow the Old Testament on this, but found the reason for God's forgiveness in the goodness of the patriarchs, see George Foot Moore, *Judaism in the First Centuries of the Christian Era* (Harvard University Press, 1954), Vol. I, pp. 535–545; and even more competently for the Tannaitic period, Erik Sjöberg, *Gott und die Sünder im palästinschen Judentum* (Stuttgart and Berlin: Kohlhammer Verlag, 1938), pp. 42–55.

6. Karl Holl, *The Distinctive Elements in Christianity,* tr. by Norman V. Hope (Edinburgh: T. & T. Clark, 1937), pp. 19 f.

7. Reference can be made in this connection to the rich collection of extra-Biblical sources dealing with this theme in Edward R. Dalglish, *Psalm Fifty-one* (Leiden: E. J. Brill, 1962).

8. Eichrodt, *op. cit.,* Vol. III, p. 136.

9. *Ibid.,* p. 138.

10. *Ibid.*, p. 139.

11. *Ibid.*, p. 140.

12. *Ibid.*, p. 141.

13. Paul Tillich, in his sermon "The Good I Will, I Do Not," *Religion in Life,* Vol. XXVIII (1959), p. 541.

14. Mowrer, *Crisis,* pp. 47–55.

15. So H.-J. Thilo in his article "Sin and Psychotherapy," *Religion in Life,* Vol. XXX (Spring, 1961), pp. 243–255. Seward Hiltner offers an interesting incident confirming that the Christian conception of sin may indeed be a fruitful area of dialogue between the behavioral sciences and theology (see "The Dialogue on Man's Nature," in *The Nature of Man,* ed. by Simon Doniger [Harper & Row, Publishers, Inc., 1961], p. 253).

16. Johannes Pedersen, *Israel: Its Life and Culture* (London: Oxford University Press, 1926), Vols. I–II, p. 411.

17. Kraus, *op. cit.,* Vol. I, p. 95.

18. Pedersen, *op. cit.,* p. 411, makes the same point.

19. So Gerhard von Rad in *Genesis, A Commentary,* tr. by John H. Marks (The Westminster Press, 1961), p. 98.

20. Pedersen, *op. cit.,* p. 414.

21. Rudolf Bultmann, *Theology of the New Testament,* tr. by Kendrick Grobel (Charles Scribner's Sons, 1951), Vol. I, p. 245.

22. E. König, cited in Quell, *"hamartanō,"* Kittel's *TWNT,* Vol. I, p. 273.

23. Norman Snaith, *The Distinctive Ideas of the Old Testament* (London: The Epworth Press, Publishers, 1944), p. 62.

24. Pedersen, *op. cit.,* p. 432.

25. *Ibid.,* p. 415.

26. *Ibid.,* p. 417.

27. *Ibid.,* pp. 418 f.

28. See the comprehensive study of the terminology and psychology of sin by Stefan Porúbčan, *Sin in the Old Testament* (Rome: Herder, 1963).

CHAPTER II

1. Stamm, *op. cit.,* p. 105.

2. On this point, see the inconclusive discussion by Stamm, *op. cit.,* pp. 57 f.

3. See on this subject especially, Richard Hentschke, *Die Stellung der vorexilischen Schriftpropheten zum Kultus* (Berlin, 1957).

4. Markus Barth, *Was Christ's Death a Sacrifice?* (*Scottish Journal of Theology*, Occasional Papers, No. 9 [Edinburgh, 1961]), p. 9.

5. Ludwig Köhler, *Old Testament Theology*, tr. by A. S. Todd (London: Lutterworth Press, 1957), p. 217. Edmond Jacob, *Theology of the Old Testament*, tr. by A. W. Heathcote and P. J. Allcock (Harper & Row, Publishers, Inc., 1958), p. 292, says *salach* has an "attenuated sense" here. Stamm, *op. cit.*, pp. 48 f., 107, and Herner, *op. cit.*, p. 22, also take this position.

6. As observed by Stamm, *op. cit.*, p. 50.

7. See Herner's discussion of this, *op. cit.*, p. 55.

8. As noted by Stamm, *op. cit.*, pp. 50 f., whose competent treatment of this theme has been summarized for the most part in this section.

9. Cf. Stamm, *op. cit.*, p. 52.

10. Cf. Herner, *op. cit.*, p. 64.

11. Stamm, *op. cit.*, p. 53.

12. Stamm, *op. cit.*, p. 54, quotes R. Kittel: "The increased consciousness of sins of later times is aware that every answer to prayer first includes within it the forgiveness of sins."

13. So Ludwig Köhler, *op. cit.*, p. 218, followed by Stamm, *op. cit.*, p. 55.

14. See Kraus, *op. cit.*, Vol. II, p. 702; Stamm, *op. cit.*, pp. 56, 78 f.

15. According to Wilhelm Bousset, the prayer of penance is a characteristic feature of the literature of the intertestamental period. We find it in I Baruch, Prayer of Manasseh, and the Prayer of Azariah. Daniel's prayer is the prototype (German, *Muster*), see Ch. IV, note 7.

16. James Barr, *The Semantics of Biblical Language* (Oxford University Press, 1961), Ch. 8.

17. The attempt by Emerson, *op. cit.*, pp. 75, 82–95, to see the meaning of "forgiveness" primarily as "lifting a weight" suffers from the same desire to narrow the meaning of "forgiveness" to his own research interests. It is correct that *salach* can mean "having a weight lifted," but it is erroneous to leave

the impression that it is either the only meaning or the most significant meaning. The broadsides Emerson fires against the work of Bultmann and the article in the *IDB* contain some truth, although both Bultmann and Quanbeck could be taken as allies by Emerson, had he taken the trouble to study them more carefully. Emerson could have made a fine contribution to the discussion between Biblical scholars and the parish if he had leveled with the scholars. For example, it is striking that Koehler and Baumgartner's *Lexicon in Veteris Testamenti Libros* (Leiden: E. J. Brill, 1953) does not even hint that *salach* occurs anywhere in the Old Testament with the meaning "lifting a weight."

18. In this section the debt to Stamm's work, *op. cit.*, pp. 66–84, is acknowledged. On technical aspects he should be consulted. His study includes the concept of redemption, while Herner, *op. cit.*, studies it in connection with atonement.

19. H. W. Wolff, *Biblischer Kommentar* XIV (*Dōdekapro-phēton*), *Hosea* (Neukirchen Kreis Moers, 1961), p. 304.

20. These psalms of imprecation have always been somewhat problematic, especially for Christian interpreters. In Ps. 109, Kraus suggests that vs. 6–20 are actually expressed not by the writer of the psalm but by the enemy of the righteous one (*op. cit.*, Vol. II, p. 751). See also Redlich, *op. cit.*, pp. 68 f.

CHAPTER III

1. See Stamm, *op. cit.*, p. 107. In this section, I acknowledge with gratitude Professor Stamm's permission to follow his outline and at times to summarize his argument.

2. Cited by Stamm, *op. cit.*, pp. 110 f.

3. Herner, *op. cit.*, pp. 52 f. In Ex. 34:9, "our iniquity" and "our sin" are an exception in the case of Moses.

4. As observed by Redlich, *op. cit.*, p. 48. Eichrodt insists that the restoration of a personal relationship stands at the center of Old Testament forgiveness, even in the cultus (*op. cit.*, Vol. III, p. 119).

5. Cited by Stamm, *op. cit.*, pp. 115 f. Wolff, *op. cit.*, p. xxii, also takes this position, noting that it is most characteristic for Hosea to announce Yahweh as drawing near in person to

execute punishment (chs. 5:12,14; 7:12,16; 12:10; 13:7 f.) and that he appears not only as avenger (chs. 4:9; 9:7; 12:2) but also as educator (*"Erzieher,"* chs. 5:2, 9; 10:10).

6. Taken from Wolff, *op. cit.*, p. xxi.

7. On the difficulties of dating and interpreting this verse, see Stamm, *op. cit.*, p. 68.

8. Herner, *op. cit.*, p. 38.

9. On the difficulties of dating and interpreting this verse, consult the commentaries.

10. George Adam Smith makes this observation in his sermon "The Forgiveness of Sins" published in the volume *The Forgiveness of Sins* (A. C. Armstrong and Son, 1904), pp. 18 f. On Isaiah, see also Martin von Gerlach, *Der Mensch im Stande der Schuld nach . . . Jesaja* (Leipzig, 1890).

11. Stamm, *op. cit.*, p. 120.

12. *Ibid.*, p. 124.

13. On this verse, Herner, *op. cit.*, p. 43, remarks, "Where there is forgiveness, there sickness does not reign."

14. See Stamm, *op. cit.*, p. 132.

15. Kraus, *op. cit.*, Vol. I, p. 384, warns that the dogma of causal connection between sickness and guilt should not be carried into every psalm.

16. The most thorough analysis and exegesis, as well as comparison with similar literary types, of Ps. 51 is provided by Dalglish, *op. cit.*

17. Kraus, *op. cit.*, p. 386, observes that violations against people are seen early as violations against God (Gen. 39:9).

18. *Pesha'* is the term used for "sin" here, which Delitzsch translates "to tear one's self away from God" and Köhler as the "raising of the human will against the will of God" (Kraus, *op. cit.*, p. 385).

19. Stamm, *op. cit.*, p. 135.

20. Snaith, *op. cit.*, p. 9.

21. *Ibid.*, p. 185.

22. Eichrodt, *op. cit.*, p. 131.

23. *Ibid.*, p. 132.

24. Jacob, *op. cit.*, p. 204.

25. *Ibid.*

26. *Ibid.*

27. See Porúbčan, *op. cit.*, pp. 287–325, on the logic and psychology of forgiveness. J. J. van As, *Skuldbelydenis en genadeverkondiging in die Ou Testament* (Utrecht, 1961), looks at the relation of man's confession and God's act.

CHAPTER IV

1. Richard Thomas Mead, "The Authority to Forgive Sins in the New Testament" (Vanderbilt Dissertation, 1960), is the best recent treatment of this material.

2. A. Büchler, *Studies in Sin and Atonement* (London, 1928), p. 1.

3. Solomon Schechter, *Some Aspects of Rabbinic Theology* (The Macmillan Company, 1909), p. 219.

4. Moore, *op. cit.*, Vol. I, pp. 461–462.

5. The most competent treatment of this theme is by Sjöberg, *op. cit.*

6. See H. Volz, "Zur Überlieferung des Gebetes Manasse," *Zeitschrift für Kirchengeschichte* 70 (1959), pp. 293–307. Luther designated it as *oratio pulcherrima omni confessuro aptissima* and recommended its use prior to confession, *Weimar Ausgabe* Deutsche Bibel 12 (1961), pp. LIX ff. According to Volz, it existed in three different German translations and more than fifty editions.

7. Wilhelm Bousset, *Die Religion des Judentums* (Berlin, 1903), p. 370.

8. So Willy Staerk, *Sünde und Gnade* (Tübingen, 1905), p. 18.

9. C. K. Barrett, ed., *The New Testament Background: Selected Documents* (London: S.P.C.K., 1956), p. 162.

10. K. G. Kuhn, *Achtzehngebet und Vaterunser und der Reim* (Tübingen, 1950), p. 10.

11. Leo Jung, *Yoma* (London: The Soncino Press, Ltd., 1938), p. xii. His introduction has a succinct description of the events of the day. I have followed it to a large extent here, and also J. C. Rylaarsdam's article in the *IDB*, Vol. I, pp. 313–316. Max Arzt, *Justice and Mercy* (Holt, Rinehart and Winston, Inc., 1963), provides a helpful commentary on the liturgy used on the Day of Atonement (pp. 191–290). The best overall

presentation is by S. Landersdorfer, "Studien zum biblischen Versöhnungstag," in *Alttestamentliche Abhandlungen,* ed. by A. Schulz (Münster, 1927), pp. 1–90.

CHAPTER V

1. M. Mansoor, *The Thanksgiving Hymns* (Wm. B. Eerdmans Publishing Company, 1961), is consistently used as our primary source.

2. J. Licht, "The Doctrine of the Thanksgiving Scroll," *Israel Exploration Journal,* Vol. VI (1956), p. 10.

3. J. Philip Hyatt, "The View of Man in the Qumran 'Hodayoth,'" *NTS,* Vol. II (1955–1956), p. 278. Herbert Braun says man is seen more negatively than in the Old Testament, "Römer 7, 7–25 und das Selbstverständnis des Qumran-Frommen," *Gesammelte Studien* (Tübingen, 1962), p. 115.

4. Mansoor, *op. cit.,* p. 189, refers to 1QS IV:21–22 and CD iii:17 where a similar expression occurs.

5. Mansoor, *op. cit.,* p. 162, citing Burrows.

6. For this last paragraph I am especially indebted to Braun's thorough study, *loc. cit.,* and to Helmer Ringgren, *The Faith of Qumran,* tr. by E. T. Sander (Fortress Press, 1963), pp. 120–126.

7. Licht, *loc. cit.,* p. 96.

8. See Manfred Weise, *Kultzeiten und kultischer Bundesschluss in der "Ordensregel" vom Toten Meer* (Leiden, 1961), pp. 61 ff., 75–82.

9. Against the sweeping generalizations made by Krister Stendahl in his otherwise excellent article, "The Apostle Paul and the Introspective Conscience of the West," in *HTR,* Vol. LVI (1963), p. 208.

CHAPTER VI

1. Mead, "The Authority to Forgive Sins," p. 11.

2. Bousset, *op. cit.,* pp. 363–364.

3. Moore, *op. cit.,* Vol. I, p. 535.

4. I. Abrahams, *Studies in Pharisaism and the Gospels,* First Series (Cambridge, 1917), p. 140. He feels that "the teaching

of Judaism on the subject of forgiveness is in fact the brightest and strongest link in its golden chain" (p. 156).

5. Schechter, *op. cit.*, p. 294.

6. Paul Billerbeck, in H. L. Strack and P. Billerbeck, *Kommentar zum Neuen Testament aus Talmud und Midrasch,* (1922–1928), Vol. I, p. 495.

7. Mead, "The Authority to Forgive Sins," p. 18.

8. S. Mowinckel, *He That Cometh,* tr. by G. W. Anderson (Abingdon Press, 1956), pp. 318–319. Also, Billerbeck, *op. cit.,* Vol. I, p. 495: "We know of no place which attributes the forgiveness of sins to the Messiah on the basis of omnipotence."

9. Sjöberg, *op. cit.,* pp. 42–71.

10. Moore, *op. cit.,* Vol. I, p. 545.

11. David Daube, *Sin, Ignorance and Forgiveness in the Bible* (Claude Montefiore Lecture, 1960 [London: Liberal Jewish Synagogue]), p. 2.

12. *Ibid.,* pp. 24 f.

13. *Ibid.,* p. 24.

14. Billerbeck, *op. cit.,* Vol. I, p. 166.

15. For these and other statements, see Billerbeck, *op. cit.,* Vol. I, pp. 162–172. See also Schechter, *op. cit.,* Ch. XVIII.

16. R. H. Charles, *The Apocrypha and Pseudepigrapha of the Old Testament* (Oxford at the Clarendon Press, 1913), Vol. II, p. 292.

17. *Ibid.,* p. 293.

CHAPTER VII

1. Agnes Smith Lewis, "Did John Preach Baptism for the Remission of Sins?" *The Expositor,* 5th Series, Vol. VII (1898), p. 226.

2. A. C. Deane, "The Ministry of John the Baptist," *The Expositor,* 8th Series, Vol. XIII (1917), p. 426.

3. Against Harald Sahlin, *Der Messias und das Gottesvolk* (Uppsala, 1945), p. 295, who follows Bultmann, *TWNT,* Vol. I, p. 507, but both are in error. *Aphesis* can best be translated here (Lev. 16:26) as "release" or "unto freedom." The Hebrew has *Azazel.*

4. Sahlin, *Der Messias,* pp. 239–295.

5. Sahlin, *Studien zum dritten Kapitel Lukas* (Uppsala, 1949), pp. 15 ff.

6. Rudolf Otto, *The Kingdom of God and the Son of Man,* tr. by F. V. Filson and B. Woolf (London: Lutterworth Press, 1938), p. 77. He believes that Jesus and John share the idea that salvation is attained through forgiveness.

7. Carl Kraeling, *John the Baptist* (Charles Scribner's Sons, 1951), p. 121. Cf. also C. H. H. Scobie, *John the Baptist* (London: SCM Press, Ltd., 1964), pp. 111 f.

8. Kraeling, *op. cit.,* p. 121.

9. *Ibid.,* p. 122.

10. The discussion of John the Baptist has increased through the discovery of the Dead Sea Scrolls. On some of the above points the best treatment is that of Joachim Jeremias, "Elijah," in *TWNT,* Vol. II, pp. 930 ff. See also Kraeling, *op. cit.,* for an excellent treatment that unfortunately could not take account of the Qumran material. The fact that Elijah was considered by the Zealots as one of their revolutionary heroes may have contributed to John's reluctance to be identified with Elijah. Treatments worth consulting that take account of the Qumran material are: J. Steinmann, *Saint John the Baptist,* tr. by M. Boyes (Harper & Row, Publishers, Inc., 1958); J. A. T. Robinson, "The Baptism of John and the Qumran Community," *Twelve New Testament Studies* (London: SCM Press, Ltd., 1962), pp. 11–27; H. H. Rowley, "The Baptism of John and the Qumran Sect," *New Testament Essays,* ed. by A. J. B. Higgins (Manchester, England: Manchester University Press, 1959), pp. 218–229; W. H. Brownlee, "John the Baptist in the New Light of Ancient Scrolls," *Interpretation,* Vol. IX (1955), pp. 71–90. Still worth consulting is A. Schlatter, *Johannes der Täufer* (Basel, 1956), which, although written in 1880, eminently deserved publication some seventy-five years later!

11. See the discussion in Büchsel, *NTD,* p. 39: "Naturally for the Evangelist everything depends upon the fact that the Baptizer spoke like this. If the Evangelist would himself have imposed these words upon him, it would be worthless, even worse than that." Both C. H. Dodd, *Interpretation of the Fourth Gospel* (London: Cambridge University Press, 1953), p. 238, and C. K. Barrett, "The Lamb of God," *NTS,* Vol. I

(1955), p. 213, agree that the expression "Lamb of God" could have been used by the Baptist.

12. On John the Baptizer, see also the excellent article by Vielhauer in *RGG³*, Vol. III, cols. 804–808.

CHAPTER VIII

1. H.-J. Kraus, *op. cit.*, *ad loc.*

2. Compare J. Schniewind, *NTD*, Vol. I¹, *ad loc.*

3. Ernst Lohmeyer, *Lord of the Temple*, tr. by S. Todd (Edinburgh: Oliver & Boyd, Ltd., 1961), p. 53.

4. William Wrede, "Zur Heilung des Gelähmten (Mc. 2:1 ff.)," *ZnW*, Vol. V (1904), p. 354.

5. *Ibid.*, p. 358.

6. Lohmeyer, *Das Evangelium Markus, ad loc.*

7. They have been competently dealt with by Mead both in his dissertation, "The Authority to Forgive Sins," and in an article, "The Healing of the Paralytic—A Literary Unit?" *JBL*, Vol. LXXX (1961), pp. 351–354.

8. M. Dibelius, *From Tradition to Gospel*, tr. by B. L. Woolf (London: Ivor Nicholson & Watson, Ltd., 1934), pp. 67–68.

9. Mead, "Healing," p. 351.

10. *Ibid.*, p. 354.

11. Wrede, *loc. cit.*, p. 355.

12. Hans Freiherr von Campenhausen, *Kirchliches Amt und geistliche Vollmacht* (Tübingen, 1953), pp. 8–11, freely translated.

13. Walter Grundmann, *"Tharsei,"* *TWNT*, Vol. III, pp. 25–27.

14. *Ibid.*, p. 26.

15. On the relation of courage and forgiveness, see Paul Tillich, *The Courage to Be* (Yale University Press, 1952), pp. 164–167. According to the manuscript D, Jesus also used this word in his reply to the criminal on the cross (Luke 23:43).

16. I am paraphrasing here the comments by A. Schlatter in *Der Evangelist Matthäus* (Stuttgart, 1957), pp. 296 ff. Cf. also, Mackintosh, *op. cit.*, pp. 88–92.

17. Schlatter, *Der Evangelist Matthäus*, p. 301.

18. Bultmann, *The History of the Synoptic Tradition,* tr. by John Marsh (Harper & Row, Publishers, Inc., 1963), pp. 15*–16*.

19. L. v. Sybel, "Die Salbungen," *ZnW*, Vol. XXIII (1924), pp. 184–193, and Bultmann, *History of the Synoptic Tradition,* pp. 20*–21*.

20. Hans Windisch, "Das Erlebnis des Sünders in den Evangelien," *Zeitschrift für Theologie und Kirche,* Vol. XXVII (1917), pp. 292–313.

21. Windisch, *loc. cit.* The sermon by Paul Tillich entitled "To Whom Much Is Forgiven" is one of the best treatments of this passage available (*The New Being* [Charles Scribner's Sons, 1955], pp. 3–14). Cf. also Mackintosh, *op. cit.,* pp. 92–94. Søren Kierkegaard's sermon on Luke 7:47 (tr. by Walter Lowrie in *For Self-examination; and, Judge for Yourselves! and Three Discourses, 1851* [Oxford University Press, 1941], pp.9–16) still repays reading.

22. So Georg Braumann, "Die Schuldner und die Sünderin in Luk. VII. 36–50," *NTS*, Vol. X (1964), pp. 487–493.

23. Windisch, *loc. cit.*

24. Windisch, *loc. cit.,* made an excellent beginning when he tried to get into the experience of the sinner who confronted Jesus, an approach skillfully used also by Mackintosh, *op. cit.,* pp. 76 ff. Jakob Haas, *Die Stellung Jesu zu Sünde und Sünder nach den vier Evangelien* (Freiburg, 1953), is strangely unaware of Windisch's work and could have profited from that approach. Haas's study is more extensive and merits consultation.

25. This is developed especially ably by A. Schlatter, *Das Evangelium Lukas* (Stuttgart, 1960), pp. 346 ff. I am indebted in the above to H. Conzelmann, *The Theology of St. Luke,* tr. by G. Buswell (Harper & Row, Publishers, Inc., 1960), pp. 225 ff.

26. Conzelmann, *op. cit.,* p. 228.

27. This is especially the conclusion reached by Ulrich Becker, *Jesus und die Ehebrecherin* (Berlin, 1963). J. D. M. Derrett has made the most careful and comprehensive study of the various aspects of the story itself in the article "Law in the New Testament: The Story of the Woman Taken in Adultery," *NTS*, Vol. X (1963), pp. 1–26.

28. Derrett, *loc. cit.*, p. 19.

29. *Ibid.*, p. 8.

30. *Ibid.*, pp. 23–24 (his italics).

31. This verse has recently been ably dealt with by Daube, "'For They Know Not What They Do': Luke 23:34," in *Studia Patristica*, Vol. IV, Part II, ed. by F. L. Cross (Berlin, 1961), pp. 58–70.

32. Mead, "The Authority to Forgive Sins," p. 104.

33. *Ibid.*, p. 142.

34. *Ibid.*, p. 259.

CHAPTER IX

1. Moore, *op. cit.*, Vol. III, p. 151.

2. William Sanday and Arthur C. Headlam, *A Critical and Exegetical Commentary on Paul's Epistle to the Romans:* "It [justification] is simply Forgiveness, Free Forgiveness" (p. 36). W. H. P. Hatch, "The Pauline Idea of Forgiveness," *Studies in Early Christianity*, ed. by S. J. Case (1928), p. 347, takes the same position.

3. So Alfred Willetts, *What the New Testament Says About Forgiveness* (Association Press, 1964), and Emerson, *op. cit.*, pp. 96 f., 127. E. Cremer, *Die Vergebung der Sünden durch Jesus* (Gütersloh, 1895), p. 8, asserts that whereas the Kingdom of God is foremost in the proclamation of Jesus, the forgiveness of sins is in the forefront of the proclamation of the apostles.

4. Among others, see Gerhard Bindemann, *Das Gebet um Vergebung der Sünden* (Gütersloh: Bertelsmann Verlag, 1902); L. Ihmels, *Die tägliche Vergebung der Sünden* (Leipzig, 1901); Paul Wernle, *Der Christ und die Sünde bei Paulus* (Leipzig, 1897).

5. Günther Harder, *Paulus und das Gebet* (Gütersloh, 1936), p. 210. Carl Schneider, "Paulus und das Gebet," *Angelos*, Vol. 4 (1932), concludes that the penitential prayer is decidedly in the background in Paul (pp. 22 ff.).

6. Harder, *op. cit.*, pp. 210 ff.

7. *Ibid.*, p. 213.

8. This has been done by both Ihmels and Bindemann in the works cited. At all costs, Ihmels especially must make Paul a good "Lutheran."

9. Hatch, *loc. cit.*, p. 341. See Stendahl, "The Apostle Paul," *loc. cit.*, p. 202. Mackintosh, *op. cit.*, pp. 111 ff., concludes that essentially Paul says the same as Jesus but the detailed expression is in terms traditional and Rabbinic in origin.

10. Stendahl, "Sünde und Schuld in Neuen Testament," *RGG*, Vol. VI, col. 487.

CHAPTER X

1. Bent Noack, "On I John II. 12–14," *NTS*, Vol. VI (1959–1960), p. 240.

2. Dodd, *The Apostolic Preaching and Its Developments* (London: Hodder & Stoughton, Ltd., 1936), pp. 23, 25, 47.

3. Other parallels are provided by Ernst Lohmeyer, *Das Vater-Unser* (Göttingen, 1962⁵), pp. 116 f.

4. See Stendahl, "Prayer and Forgiveness," *Svensk Exegetisk Arsbok*, Vols. XXII–XXIII (1957–1958), pp. 75–86, especially p. 75.

5. *Ibid.*, p. 77.

6. Bultmann, *History of the Synoptic Tradition*, p. 54, cites Mark 11:20–25 as one passage in which "there are compelling grounds for supposing that an originally independent dominical saying was subsequently provided with a setting."

7. Stendahl, "Prayer and Forgiveness," p. 78.

8. So St. Peter Chrysologus (ca. 406–450), cited in C. M. O'Donnell, *St. Cyprian on the Lord's Prayer* (The Catholic University of America Press, 1960), p. 25.

9. See R. Pettazzoni, "Confession of Sins: An Attempted General Interpretation," in R. Pettazzoni, *Essays on the History of Religions*, tr. by H. J. Rose (Leiden: E. J. Brill, 1954), pp. 43–54.

10. *Ibid.*, p. 45.

11. *Ibid.*, p. 49.

12. Pettazzoni, "Confession of Sins and the Classics," *Essays*, p. 67. Although a sense of sin does not pervade the classics, Pettazzoni calls our attention to a striking passage in Ovid: "I too repent! O, if any wretched man is believed in anything, I too repent! I feel the torture of my own deed! Though exile is anguish, greater anguish is my fault and it is a smaller thing

to suffer the punishment than to have deserved it. What though the gods and he who is more conspicuous than the gods should favour me, my punishment can be removed, my fault will remain for ever. Death at least by his coming will put an end to my exile, my sin even death will not remove" (*Ex Ponto*, Vol. I, i, pp. 59–60, Loeb Classical Library).

13. So A. E. Wilhelm-Hooijbergh, *Peccatum, Sin and Guilt in Ancient Rome* (Groningen, 1954), pp. 89, 91.

14. Reinhold Seeberg, *Die Sünden und die Sündenvergebung nach dem ersten Brief des Johannes, Festschrift für L. Ihmels* (Leipzig, 1928), says that if we have here more than merely an inner penitent attitude, "then we have here one of the earliest witnesses to a churchly practice of confession" (*eine Kirchliche Beichte*), (p. 22).

15. Rudolf Schnackenburg, *Die Johannesbriefe* (Verlag Herder, Freiburg, 1953), p. 75 lists a number of people who have taken this position.

16. Erich Haupt, *The First Epistle of St. John*, tr. by W. B. Pope (Edinburgh, 1879), p. 46.

17. Billerbeck, *op. cit.*, Vol. I, p. 170.

18. *Ibid.*

19. Dodd, *The Johannine Epistles* (London: Hodder & Stoughton, Inc., 1946), pp. 22 ff.

20. *Ibid.*

21. Schnackenburg, *op. cit.*, p. 76, in his otherwise excellent discussion seems to stress too little the involvement of the congregation. If, as he correctly stresses, forgiveness is a personal divine act, how does God perform this act? Emerson, in spite of some things he says about forgiveness being mediated through community, still equivocates on the issue. It is simply not true that "in the New Testament, and particularly in the epistles, the mediation is not so much by a group as by a person—Jesus Christ" (*op. cit.*, p. 87). Nor should we distinguish between forgiveness on an individual basis or in relation to other people (p. 165). The New Testament sees the church as the embodiment of Christ; thus we can no longer see forgiveness as some mystical influence or feeling or energy transmitted across the ethereal waves—nor can the individual and communal aspects of forgiveness be separated.

22. Mark provides an interesting case of relating the two when he deviates from the LXX in his quotation of Isa. 6:10 in ch. 4:12. Where it occurs elsewhere (Matt. 13:15; John 12:40; Acts 28:27), the word "heal" occurs. In Mark alone the word "forgive" appears (cf. Heb. 12:13).

23. Visiting the sick was also highly praised and much practiced in Judaism; see Billerbeck, *op. cit.*, Vol. IV, 1, pp. 573 ff. On the importance of the (deathly) sick confessing their sins, see Billerbeck, *op. cit.*, Vol. I, pp. 113 ff., and Vol. IV, 1, pp. 576 f.

24. Dibelius, *Der Brief des Jakobus* (Göttingen, 1959), p. 233.

25. J. B. Mayor, *The Epistle of St. James* (London, 1913), pp. 170–173, provides a rich collection of material on the place of oil in the early church and in later church history. On the subject of healing, I refer the reader to my forthcoming book *The Healing Community.*

26. Paul Althaus, "Bekenne einer dem andern seine Sünden," *Zahn Festgabe* (Leipzig, 1928), pp. 165–194.

27. Max Thurian, *Confession,* tr. by E. Hudson (London: SCM Press, Ltd., 1958), p. 84.

28. Conzelmann, *op. cit.*, p. 179, accepts Bornkamm's suggestion that for Luke, blasphemy against the Son may be forgivable, because it is not until Pentecost that it is revealed who he is. Luke does indicate that the time of ignorance is an excuse for rejection.

29. G. B. Caird, *The Gospel of St. Luke* (Penguin Books Inc., 1963), p. 161.

30. H. W. Beyer, *"blasphēmeō"* in *TWNT*, Vol. I, p. 624.

31. Schlatter, *Der Evangelist Matthäus*, p. 408.

32. The Greek word *paradeigmatizō*, "hold him up to contempt," used here is also used by the LXX translators in Num. 25:4, where a case of public exhibition is involved.

33. Seeberg, *op. cit.*, pp. 27 ff.

34. I am summarizing here the argument of Seeberg, *op. cit.*, pp. 27–30.

35. Schnackenburg, *loc. cit.*, p. 248.

36. *Ibid.*, p. 249.

37. Epistle 185:49 (tr. by J. A. King, Nicene Fathers, Series 1, 4).

CHAPTER XI

1. Martin Marty, *The New Shape of American Religion* (Harper & Row, Publishers, Inc., 1958), p. 144.

2. Geddes MacGregor, *Corpus Christi* (The Westminster Press, 1958), p. 249.

3. Geddes MacGregor, *The Coming Reformation* (The Westminster Press, 1960), Ch. 4.

4. John Kennedy, *Presbyterian Authority and Discipline* (Edinburgh: St. Andrew Press, 1960), p. 77.

5. Karl Barth, *Die kirchliche Dogmatik*, Vol. IV, Part 1 (1953), pp. 779 f.

6. *Ibid.*, Vol. IV, Part 2, pp. 804 f.

7. Eduard Thurneysen, *A Theology of Pastoral Care*, tr. by J. Worthington, *et al.* (John Knox Press, 1962), Ch. 2.

8. Bultmann, *Theology of the New Testament*, Vol. II, pp. 231–236.

9. Gerhard Ebeling, *Kirchenzucht* (Stuttgart: Kohlhammer, 1947), p. 9.

10. *Ibid.*, p. 59.

11. Ruth Götze, *Wie Luther Kirchenzucht übte* (Göttingen, 1958).

12. See Götze, *op. cit.*, p. 104. Roger Ley, *Kirchenzucht bei Zwingli* (Zurich, 1948), has not only documented this point with reference to Zwingli but also tried to defend it.

13. Helen von Freyburg's written confession is a part of the recently discovered *Kunstbuch;* see Heinold Fast, "Das oberdeutsche Täufertum, Ein neuer Handschriftenfund," *Archiv für Reformationsgeschichte*, Vol. 47 (1956), pp. 212–242.

14. Rudolf Bohren, *Das Problem der Kirchenzucht im Neuen Testament* (Zurich, 1952).

15. R. A. Raines, *New Life in the Church* (Harper & Row, Publishers, Inc., 1961), deals with discipline in Ch. VI (pp. 55–64) and sees discipline as the "grooves of grace" (p. 59). Although I agree that when these are dug deep, "they become channels to release God's power for living the new life in Christ," my concern in the present study is more with discipline than with disciplines.

16. Bohren, *op. cit.*, p. 15.

17. Bultmann, *Theology*, Vol. II, pp. 231 f.

18. Thurneysen, *op. cit.*, p. 36.

19. MacGregor, *The Coming Reformation*, p. 65.

20. In this connection, see J. H. Bavinck's article "Kirchen-zucht in den jungen Kirchen," *RGG*³, Vol. III, cols. 1603–1605.

21. Bavinck, *loc. cit.*, col. 1603.

22. Snaith, *op. cit.*, p. 180. The idea is more fully developed in *ET*, Vol. 57 (1945), pp. 47 f.

23. Johannes Behm, *TWNT*, Vol. V, p. 802, footnote 30.

24. See Otto Schmitz, *TWNT*, Vol. V, pp. 792–794.

25. *Parakaleō* is used here, but the KJV "beseech" and RSV and NEB "make an appeal" are not as accurate as Luther's *"Gott vermahnet durch uns."* Schmitz also comments, "One will need to prefer *'ermahnen'*, for the weight of the authority is in question here and this authority is active in the word of the proclaimer."

26. See the words quoted from Schlatter in Schmitz, *loc. cit.*, p. 793.

27. Kierkegaard, *op. cit.*, p. 11. I regard it as the fundamental error of Paul Tournier's *Guilt and Grace* (London: Hodder & Stoughton, Ltd., 1962) that he has not captured the Biblical stress on the healing side of judgment (see his Part II, "The Spirit of Judgment," and in particular Ch. XI, "Judgment Is Destructive").

28. Büchsel, *TWNT*, Vol. II, pp. 470 ff.

29. So Bertram, *TWNT*, Vol. II, p. 471.

30. Moore, *op. cit.*, Vol. II, pp. 152 ff.

31. *Ibid.*, pp. 147 ff. Otto Betz, *Der Paraklet* (Leiden/Köln: E. J. Brill, 1963), has collected much material on the place of rebuke and admonition in the Qumran sect and also its implications for the understanding of the role of the Paraclete in the New Testament (see pp. 106–116 and pp. 192–206).

32. With the Nestle Greek text and the New English Bible, the words "against you" must be dropped as a later addition. The manuscript witnesses are divided and thus not decisive. On the ground of the shorter and harder reading, it is preferred. Even if one accepts the longer reading, Luke 17:3 and Lev. 19:17 agree in omitting the specific words "against you."

33. Paul S. Minear, *Eyes of Faith* (The Westminster Press, 1946), p. 75.

34. Hiltner, "The Defining of Pastoral Theology," *Religion in Life,* Vol. XXVIII (1959), p. 499.

35. Both the Manual of Discipline and the Damascus Document prohibit bringing an accusation by a member against his fellow without first having reproved him before two witnesses (1QS v:24–vi:1; CD ix:2–8). H van Vliet, *No Single Testimony* (Utrecht, 1958), traces the adoption of Deut. 19:15 by the New Testament writers.

36. See Behm, *"noutheteō," TWNT,* Vol. IV, pp. 1013–1016, to which this treatment is indebted.

37. The NEB offers an interesting example of reading a modern concept into the translation when it renders *noutheteō* "counsel" in this verse. In I Thess. 5:12 the word "counsellors" appears, and the word is translated "give friendly advice" in II Thess. 3:15 and as "give advice to one another" in Rom. 15:14. This is a lamentable translation because it dilutes the lofty sense of mission felt by Paul. A similar instance can be seen in Rom. 15:25, where Paul's sense of mission is changed by the NEB to make him an errand boy!

38. The word "interpersonal" apparently comes from Harry Stack Sullivan. For a study of forgiveness as applied to this theory and compared with Emil Brunner's view on forgiveness, see S. T. Jacobson, "Forgiveness as Seen in the Writings of Harry Stack Sullivan and Emil Brunner" (Princeton Theological Seminary Dissertation, 1959).

CHAPTER XII

1. Freud, *Civilization and Its Discontents* (1930), SE, Vol. XXI, p. 134.

2. Cf. his remarks on God's kindness and the sentence "One sinned, and then one made a sacrifice or did penance and then one was free to sin once more" (*The Future of an Illusion,* SE, Vol. XXI, p. 37), as well as his comments about his own father in *The Interpretation of Dreams,* SE, Vol. IV, p. 197. On the subject of Freud's attitude toward religion, Philip Rieff's *Freud: The Mind of the Moralist* (The Viking Press, Inc., 1959), Ch. VIII, is relevant. Bernard Shaw also felt that

"forgiveness is the beggar's refuge; we must pay our debts" (Mackintosh, *op. cit.*, p. 211).

3. *Psychoanalysis and Faith: Letters Between Sigmund Freud and Oskar Pfister*, ed. by H. Meng and E. L. Freud (Basic Books, Inc., Publishers, 1963), p. 125.

4. *Ibid.*, p. 134.

5. Otto Fenichel, *The Psychoanalytic Theory of Neurosis* (W. W. Norton & Company, Inc., 1945), p. 138. He makes frequent use of the term.

6. Tillich, *The New Being*, p. 12.

7. Albert Ellis, "There Is No Place for the Concept of Sin in Psychotherapy," *Journal of Counseling Psychology*, Vol. VII (1960), pp. 191–192.

8. This is evident from the fact that Christianity did not adopt the common Greek word for forgiveness, *sungnōmē*, which means literally to "share an opinion" or to make a concession. With a deeper view of sin comes also a deeper sense of forgiveness (on this see Bultmann, *"sungnōmē* in *TWNT*, Vol. I, pp. 716 f.).

9. For a good discussion on the difference between pardoning and excusing and the limitations of "understanding," see S. Behn, "Über Vergebung und Entschuldigung," *Archiv für die gesamte Psychologie*, Vol. 86 (1932), pp. 55–62.

10. Jacobson, *op. cit.*, pp. 161–162.

11. Andras Angyal, "The Convergence of Psychotherapy and Religion," *Journal of Pastoral Care*, Vol. V (1952), p. 10.

Another excellent treatment of forgiveness from a psychiatric point of view is the article by E. Mansell Pattison, "On the Failure to Forgive or to Be Forgiven," *American Journal of Psychotherapy*, Vol. XIX (January, 1965), pp. 106–115. Pattison is especially perceptive in his analysis of the limitations of confession, the place of restitution, and his delineation of the punitive model of forgiveness over against the reconciliation model. He does not feel that forgiveness is a super ego phenomenon (p. 109).

12. *Ibid.*, pp. 12 ff.

13. Tillich, "The Eternal Now," in *The Meaning of Death*, ed. by Herman Feifel (McGraw-Hill Book Company, Inc., 1959), pp. 35 ff.

14. Does not Anna Karenina's husband experience this? He leaves her sickbed after he has discovered her unfaithfulness with the words "I have seen her and forgiven her. And the joy of forgiveness has revealed to me what my duty is . . . . I only pray that God may not take away from me the joy of forgiving." His subsequent behavior hardly speaks of forgiveness (Leo Tolstoy, *Anna Karenina*, Part IV, end of Ch. XVII).

15. Abigail Van Buren, "My Problem and How I Solved It," *Good Housekeeping* (March, 1963), pp. 10–18.

16. *McCall's* (January, 1963), p. 103.

17. See the interesting case study presented by Lawrence Kubie and H. A. Israel, in which the turn toward health in a five-year-old girl bordering on psychosis took place when each member of the clinical team said to her, "I'm sorry," in the article, "Say You're Sorry," *The Psychoanalytic Study of the Child*, Vol. X (1955), pp. 289–299.

18. Vincent Taylor, *Forgiveness and Reconciliation* (London: Macmillan & Co., Ltd., 1941), has made this point convincingly.

19. Joseph Burnaby, *Christian Words and Christian Meanings* (Harper & Row, Publishers, Inc., 1955), p. 87.

20. Paul Lehmann, *Forgiveness: Decisive Issue in Protestant Thought* (Harper & Row, Publishers, Inc., 1940), pp. 81 ff. Mackintosh says "it is more than doubtful whether in any real sense a Christian can ever 'forgive himself' for wrongdoing" (*op. cit.*, pp. 74, 89).

21. Thurneysen, *op. cit.*, p. 67.

22. Daniel Day Williams, *The Minister and the Care of Souls* (Harper & Row, Publishers, Inc., 1961), in his incisive chapter on "Forgiveness, Judgment and Acceptance," states that "psychological acceptance and the Gospel of forgiveness meet in the work of the Christian pastor" (p. 92).

CHAPTER XIII

1. James Stewart, *A Faith to Proclaim* (London: Hodder & Stoughton, Ltd., 1953), in the chapter entitled "Proclaiming Forgiveness" (p. 75).

2. Emerson's purpose, to demonstrate the essential place of forgiveness in theological thought and to show the essential place of forgiveness in making the parish relevant (*op. cit.*, p. 11), coincides closely with mine, but we have approached our subject from quite different perspectives. My study does not permit the conclusion: " 'Realized forgiveness' is at the heart of the Scripture" (p. 76).

3. Barth, *Credo* (London: Hodder & Stoughton, Ltd., 1936), p. 45.

4. Mowrer, "The Almighty's Unmighty Ministers," *The Christian Century* (Oct. 17, 1962), p. 1254.

5. Mowrer, *Crisis*, p. 196.

6. Even Mowrer's latest book represents no advance in this regard. See *The New Group Therapy* (D. Van Nostrand Company, Inc., 1964), pp. 31, 52, 107.

7. Mackintosh, *op. cit.*, pp. 269–286.

8. Adolf von Harnack, *Ausgewählte Reden und Aufsätze* (Berlin, 1951), pp. 71–73.

9. The book by E. Zellweger, *Beichte und Vergebung* (Basel: Reinhardt Verlag, 1960), gives evidence of the widespread interest in continental Europe on this question. Most remarkable is the practice of confession at the Taizé community, and any Protestant who has reservations about confession ought to study the excellent treatment by Max Thurian, *op. cit.*

10. The remarkable chapter by Max Thurian on "The Confessor," in his book *Confession* provides abundant food for reflection for Protestants who feel uneasy in this kind of posture.

11. John Wren-Lewis cited by J. A. T. Robinson in *Honest to God* (The Westminster Press, 1963), pp. 62 f.

Bibliography

BOOKS

Abrahams, I., *Studies in Pharisaism and the Gospels,* First Series. Cambridge, 1917.

Arzt, Max, *Justice and Mercy: Commentary on the Liturgy of the New Year and the Day of Atonement.* Holt, Rinehart and Winston, Inc., 1963.

Barth, Markus, *Was Christ's Death a Sacrifice?* (*Scottish Journal of Theology,* Occasional Papers, No. 9), Edinburgh, 1961.

Becker, Ulrich, *Jesus und die Ehebrecherin.* Berlin, 1963.

Bindemann, Gerhard, *Das Gebet um Vergebung der Sünden.* Gütersloh: Bertelsmann Verlag, 1902.

Bohren, Rudolf, *Das Problem der Kirchenzucht im Neuen Testament.* Zurich, 1952.

Bousset, Wilhelm, *Die Religion des Judentums.* Berlin, 1903.

Büchler, A., *Studies in Sin and Atonement.* London, 1928.

Bultmann, Rudolf, *The History of the Synoptic Tradition,* tr. by John Marsh. Harper & Row, Publishers, Inc., 1963.

———— *Theology of the New Testament,* tr. by Kendrick Grobel. 2 vols. Charles Scribner's Sons, 1951.

Campenhausen, Hans Freiherr von, *Kirchliches Amt und geistliche Vollmacht.* Tübingen, 1953.

Conzelmann, H., *The Theology of St. Luke,* tr. by G. Buswell. Harper & Row, Publishers, Inc., 1960.

Cremer, E., *Die Vergebung der Sünden durch Jesus.* Gütersloh, 1895.

Dalglish, Edward R., *Psalm Fifty-one.* Leiden: E. J. Brill, 1962.

Daube, David, *Sin, Ignorance and Forgiveness in the Bible.* Claude Montefiore Lecture; London: Liberal Jewish Synagogue, 1960.

Ebeling, Gerhard, *Kirchenzucht.* Stuttgart: Kohlhammer, 1947.

Eichrodt, Walther, *Theologie des Alten Testaments,* Vols. I–IV. Leipzig, 1939 ff.

Emerson, James G., Jr., *The Dynamics of Forgiveness.* The Westminster Press, 1964.

Fenichel, Otto, *The Psychoanalytic Theory of Neurosis.* W. W. Norton & Company, Inc., 1945.

Frank, J., *Persuasion and Healing.* The Johns Hopkins Press, 1961.

Galtier, Paul, *L'Église et la remission des peches aux premiers siècles.* Paris, 1932.

Gerlach, Martin von, *Der Mensch im Stande der Schuld nach dem Buche Jesaja.* Leipzig, 1890.

Greeves, Frederic, *Theology and the Cure of Souls.* Channel Press, Inc., 1962.

Haas, Jakob, *Die Stellung Jesu zu Sünde und Sünder nach den vier Evangelien.* Freiburg, 1953.

Harder, Günther, *Paulus und das Gebet.* Gütersloh, 1936.

Hentschke, Richard, *Die Stellung der vorexilischen Schriftpropheten zum Kultus.* Berlin, 1957.

Herner, Sven, *Sühne und Vergebung in Israel.* Lund, 1942.

Hofmann, Hans, *Religion and Mental Health.* Harper & Row, Publishers, Inc., 1961.

Holl, Karl, *The Distinctive Elements in Christianity,* tr. by Norman V. Hope. Edinburgh: T. & T. Clark, 1937.

Ihmels, L., *Die tägliche Vergebung der Sünden.* Leipzig, 1901.

Jacob, Edmond, *Theology of the Old Testament,* tr. by A. W. Heathcote and P. J. Allcock. Harper & Row, Publishers, Inc., 1958.

Jung, Leo, *Yoma.* London: The Soncino Press, Ltd., 1938.

Knox, Wilfred L., *Penitence and Forgiveness.* London, 1953.

Köberle, J., *Sünde und Gnade in religiösen Leben des Volkes Israel bis auf Christum.* München, 1905.

Köhler, Ludwig, *Old Testament Theology,* tr. by A. S. Todd. London: Lutterworth Press, 1957.

Kraeling, Carl, *John the Baptist.* Charles Scribner's Sons, 1951.

Kuhn, K. G., *Achtzehngebet und Vaterunser und der Reim.* Tübingen, 1950.

Lehmann, Paul, *Forgiveness: Decisive Issue in Protestant Thought.* Harper & Row, Publishers, Inc., 1940.

Lohmeyer, Ernst, *Das Vater-Unser.* Göttingen, 1962⁵.

Mackintosh, H. R., *The Christian Experience of Forgiveness.* London: James Nisbet & Co., Ltd., 1927.

Mansoor, M., *The Thanksgiving Hymns.* Wm. B. Eerdmans Publishing Company, 1961.

Meng, H., and Freud, E. L., editors, *Psychoanalysis and Faith: Letters Between Sigmund Freud and Oskar Pfister.* Basic Books, Inc., Publishers, 1963.

Menninger, Karl, *Theory of Psychoanalytic Technique.* Basic Books, Inc., Publishers, 1958.

Moore, George Foot, *Judaism in the First Centuries of the Christian Era,* 3 vols. Harvard University Press, 1954.

Mowinckel, S., *He That Cometh,* tr. by G. W. Anderson. Abingdon Press, 1954.

Mowrer, O. Hobart, *The Crisis in Psychiatry and Religion.* D. Van Nostrand Company, Inc., 1961.

—— *The New Group Therapy.* D. Van Nostrand Company, Inc., 1964.

Otto, Rudolf, *The Kingdom of God and the Son of Man,* tr. by F. V. Filson and B. Woolf. London: Lutterworth Press, 1938.

Palmer, P. F., *Sacraments and Forgiveness.* The Newman Press, 1959.

Pedersen, Johannes, *Israel: Its Life and Culture.* 4 vols. London: Oxford University Press, 1926.

Porúbčan, Stefan, *Sin in the Old Testament.* Rome: Herder, 1963.

Rad, Gerhard von, *Genesis, A Commentary,* tr. by John H. Marks. The Westminster Press, 1961.

Redlich, E. B., *The Forgiveness of Sins*. Edinburgh: T. & T. Clark, 1937.

Ringgren, Helmer, *The Faith of Qumran*, tr. by E. T. Sander. Fortress Press, 1963.

Sahlin, Harald, *Der Messias und das Gottesvolk*. Uppsala, 1945.

────── *Studien zum dritten Kapitel Lukas*. Uppsala, 1949.

Schechter, Solomon, *Some Aspects of Rabbinic Theology*. The Macmillan Company, 1909.

Schlatter, A., *Johannes der Täufer*. Basel, 1956.

Schulhof, J. J., *The Law of Forgiveness as Presented in the New Testament*. Cambridge, 1901.

Sjöberg, Erik, *Gott und die Sünder im palästinischen Judentum*. Stuttgart and Berlin: Kohlhammer Verlag, 1938.

Smith, George Adam, *The Forgiveness of Sins*. A. C. Armstrong and Son, 1904.

Snaith, Norman, *The Distinctive Ideas of the Old Testament*. London: The Epworth Press, Publishers, 1944.

Splittgerber, A., *Die Sünde wider den heiligen Geist, die Verstockungssünde der Wiedergeborenen*. Gütersloh, 1890.

Staerk, Willy, *Sünde und Gnade*. Tübingen, 1905.

Stamm, J. J., *Erlösen und Vergeben im Alten Testament*. Bern, 1940.

Steinmann, J., *Saint John the Baptist*, tr. by M. Boyes. Harper & Row, Publishers, Inc., 1958.

Stewart, James, *A Faith to Proclaim*. London: Hodder & Stoughton, Ltd., 1953.

Swete, H. B., *The Forgiveness of Sins*. The Macmillan Company, 1916.

Taylor, Vincent, *Forgiveness and Reconciliation*. London: Macmillan & Co., Ltd., 1941.

Telfer, William, *The Forgiveness of Sins*. Muhlenberg Press, 1960.

Thurian, Max, *Confession*, tr. by E. Hudson. London: SCM Press, Ltd., 1958.

Thurneysen, Eduard, *A Theology of Pastoral Care*, tr. by J. Worthington, *et al*. John Knox Press, 1962.

Tillich, Paul, *The Courage to Be*. Yale University Press, 1952.

Wernle, Paul, *Der Christ und die Sünde bei Paulus*. Leipzig, 1897.

White, Douglas, *Forgiveness and Suffering*. London, 1913.

Wilhelm-Hooijbergh, A. E., *Peccatum, Sin and Guilt in Ancient Rome*. Groningen, 1954.

Willetts, Alfred, *What the New Testament Says About Forgiveness*. Association Press, 1964.

Williams, Charles, *He Came Down from Heaven; and, The Forgiveness of Sins*. London: Faber & Faber, Inc., 1950.

Williams, Daniel Day, *The Minister and the Care of Souls*. Harper & Row, Publishers, Inc., 1961.

Zellweger, E., *Beichte und Vergebung*. Basel: Reinhardt Verlag, 1960.

ARTICLES

Althaus, Paul, "Bekenne einer dem andern seine Sünden," *Zahn Festgabe* (Leipzig, 1928), pp. 165–194).

Bavinck, J. H., "Kirchenzucht in den jungen Kirchen," *RGG*[3], Vol. III, cols. 1603–1605.

Behn, S., Über Vergebung und Entschuldigung," *Archiv für die gesamte Psychologie*, Vol. 86 (1932), pp. 55–62.

Braun, Herbert, "Römer 7, 7–25 und das Selbstverständnis des Qumran-Frommen," *Gesammelte Studien* (Tübingen, 1962), pp. 100–119.

Brownlee, W. H., "John the Baptist in the New Light of Ancient Scrolls," *Interpretation*, Vol. IX (1955), pp. 71–90.

Bultmann, Rudolf, "*sungnōmē*," *TWNT*, Vol. I, pp. 716–717.

——, "*aphiēmi, aphesis*," *TWNT*, Vol. I, pp. 506–508.

Catanzaro, C. J. de, "Forgiveness in the Old Testament," *American Church Quarterly*, Vol. II (1962), pp. 26–39.

Daube, David, " 'For They Know Not What They Do': Luke 23:34," *Studia Patristica*, Vol. IV, Part II, ed. by F. L. Cross (Berlin, 1961), pp. 58–70.

Derrett, J. D. M., "Law in the New Testament: The Story of the Woman Taken in Adultery," *NTS*, Vol. X (1963), pp. 1–26.

Ellis, Albert, "There Is No Place for the Concept of Sin in Psychotherapy," *Journal of Counseling Psychology*, Vol. VII (1960), pp. 191–192.

Grundmann, Walter, "*Tharsei*," *TWNT*, Vol. III, pp. 25–27.

Haroutunian, Joseph, "Grace and Freedom Reconsidered," *Journal of Religion*, Vol. XL (1960), pp. 59–79.

Hatch, W. H. P., "The Pauline Idea of Forgiveness," *Studies in Early Christianity*, ed. by S. J. Case (1928).

Hyatt, J. Philip, "The View of Man in the Qumran 'Hodayoth,'" *NTS*, Vol. II (1955–1956), pp. 276–284.

Jacobson, S. T., "Forgiveness as Seen in the Writings of Harry Stack Sullivan and Emil Brunner." Princeton Theological Seminary Dissertation, 1959.

Licht, J., "The Doctrine of the Thanksgiving Scroll," *Israel Exploration Journal*, Vol. VI (1956), pp. 1–13; 89–101.

Lohse, E., "Sünde und Schuld in Judentum," *RGG*[3], Vol. VI, cols. 482–484.

Mead, Richard Thomas, "The Authority to Forgive Sins in the New Testament." Vanderbilt Dissertation, May, 1960.

——— "The Healing of the Paralytic—a Literary Unit?" *JBL*, Vol. LXXX (1961), pp. 351–354.

Mowrer, O. Hobart, "The Almighty's Unmighty Ministers," *The Christian Century* (Oct. 17, 1962), pp. 1252–1254.

Pattison, E. Mansell, "On the Failure to Forgive or to Be Forgiven," *American Journal of Psychotherapy*, Vol. XIX (January, 1965), pp. 106–115.

Pettazzoni, R., "Confession of Sins: An Attempted General Interpretation," *Essays on the History of Religions*, tr. by H. J. Rose (Leiden: E. J. Brill, 1954), pp. 43–54.

Quanbeck, W. A., "Forgiveness," *IDB*, Vol. II, pp. 314–319.

Robinson, J. A. T., "The Baptism of John and the Qumran Community," *Twelve New Testament Studies* (London: SCM Press, Ltd., 1962), pp. 11–27.

Rowley, H. H., "The Baptism of John and the Qumran Sect," *New Testament Essays*, ed. by A. J. B. Higgins (Manchester, England: Manchester University Press, 1959), pp. 218–229.

Rylaarsdam, J. C., "Day of Atonement," *IDB*, Vol. I, pp. 313–316.

Seeberg, Reinhold, *Die Sünden und die Sündenvergebung nach dem ersten Brief des Johannes, Festschrift für L. Ihmels*, Leipzig (1928), pp. 19–31.

Stendahl, Krister, "The Apostle Paul and the Introspective Conscience of the West," *HTR*, Vol. LVI (1963), pp. 199–215.

Stendahl, Krister, "Sünde und Schuld im Neuen Testament," *RGG*, Vol. VI, cols. 484–489.

—— "Prayer and Forgiveness," *Svensk Exegetisk Årsbok*, Vols. XXII–XXIII (1957–1958), pp. 75–86.

Thilo, H.-J., "Sin and Psychotherapy," *Religion in Life*, Vol. XXX (Spring, 1961), pp. 243–255.

Tillich, Paul, "The Eternal Now," *The Meaning of Death*, ed. by Herman Feifel (McGraw-Hill Book Company, Inc., 1959), pp. 30–38.

—— "The Good I Will, I Do Not," *Religion in Life*, Vol. XXVIII (1959), pp. 539–545.

—— "To Whom Much Is Forgiven," *The New Being* (Charles Scribner's Sons, 1955), pp. 3–14.

Vielhauer, P., "Johannes der Täufer," *RGG*³, Vol. III, cols. 804–808.

Vriezen, Th. C., "Sünde und Schuld im Alten Testament," *RGG*³, Vol. VI, cols. 478–482.

Windisch, Hans, "Das Erlebnis des Sünders in den Evangelien," *Zeitschrift für Theologie und Kirche*, Vol. XXVII (1917), pp. 292–313.

Worden, T., "The Remission of Sins," *Scripture*, Vol. IX (1957), pp. 65–79; 115–127.

Wrede, William, "Zur Heilung des Gelähmten (Mc. 2:1 ff.)," *ZnW*, Vol. V (1904), pp. 354–358.